CW01266748

From the
Out House
to the
In House

Dr. Mary Ann
Gibson, Ed.D.

From the Out House *to the* In House

I Kept My Promise

PALMETTO
PUBLISHING
Charleston, SC
www.PalmettoPublishing.com

From the Out House to the In House
Copyright © 2023 by Dr. Mary Ann Gibson, Ed.D.

All rights reserved
No portion of this book may be reproduced, stored in a retrieval system, or transmitted in any form by any means–electronic, mechanical, photocopy, recording, or other– except for brief quotations in printed reviews, without prior permission of the author.

First Edition

Hardcover ISBN: 979-8-8229-2741-4
Paperback ISBN: 979-8-8229-2742-1
eBook ISBN: 979-8-8229-2743-8

This book is dedicated to the Gibson family:
To my daughters Carlo and Abria and my son Tony;
To all my grandchildren and great-grandchildren.
To all the people who have touched my life.
To ALL MY STUDENTS who have given me a
chance to show just how much I love them.
To my goddaughters and godsons.
To all my relatives and friends.

As stated in the lyric of Jason Nelson:
"Forever is a long time and that's how long I'll love you—forever."

Table of Contents

Introduction. i
Chapter One: Born During the Jim Crow Era 1
Chapter Two: Parents Meeting. 7
Chapter Three: Gib and Fiona. 9
Chapter Four: Sang it, Fiona! 12
Chapter Five: Boundaries and a Sense of Peace and Harmony 15
Chapter Six: Dancing, Togetherness, and a Pig 17
Chapter Seven: A Child of Sharecroppers 21
Chapter Eight: Mr. Oliver and a Nightmare. 24
Chapter Nine: The End of Segregation and a
        Troubling Graduation 29
Chapter Ten: Chuck, Jimmy, and the Irish Potato 35
Chapter Eleven: Jason, Castor Oil, and a Mean Neighbor 45
Chapter Twelve: Favorite Uncles 48
Chapter Thirteen: The Family Bicycle 51
Chapter Fourteen: Minnie's Thrilling Ride 53
Chapter Fifteen: Easter Sunday and the Christmas Play 56
Chapter Sixteen: Murphy the Trickster 59
Chapter Seventeen: Pranksters Catherine and Dallis 61
Chapter Eighteen: The Tithes Story 65
Chapter Nineteen: For the Love of Baseball 69

Chapter Twenty: Saying Goodbye to Daddy 72
Chapter Twenty-One: Larry the Catcher 74
Chapter Twenty-Two: Donnie and Murphy: Baseball
                Domination 76
Chapter Twenty-Three: Rita, My Angel 78
Chapter Twenty-Four: Chuck's Prized Possession. 80
Chapter Twenty-Five: The Family Huntsmen 82
Chapter Twenty-Six: (Paternal) Grandpa Sam and
                Grandma Molly 86
Chapter Twenty-Seven: Aunt Fanny 91
Chapter Twenty-Eight: Lola's Sweaters 94
Chapter Twenty-Nine: Grandma Gertrude, Moonshine,
                and Big Joe 96
Chapter Thirty: Early Career and Casey's Support 99
Chapter Thirty-One: A Janitor, a Maid 105
Chapter Thirty-Two: Help! Call the Police! 107
Chapter Thirty-Three: Twiggs County and
                Professional Challenges 110
Chapter Thirty-Four: Educational Philosophy 116
Chapter Thirty-Five: The Not-So-Good Things
                About Teaching 118
Chapter Thirty-Six: Support For New Teachers. 122
Chapter Thirty-Seven: Epilogue 126

Introduction

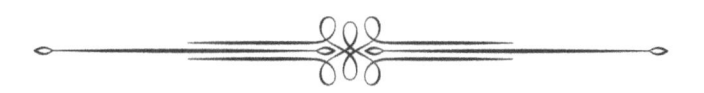

Welcome to Taylor County, Georgia, a county named after the twelfth President of the United States, Zachary Taylor.

As a General in the United States Army, Taylor became widely known due to his success in the Battle of Buena Vista during the Mexican-American War in 1847.

With only five thousand soldiers under his command, General Taylor notably defeated twenty thousand enemy soldiers led by General Antonio López de Santa Anna of the Mexican Army.

The eventual victory of the United States led to the signing of the Treaty of Guadalupe Hidalgo in 1848, which compelled Mexico to give up a considerable amount of its territory to the United States.

In the early twentieth century, Taylor County was also widely known for its history of racism and its Jim-Crow-era subjugation of Black Americans. The county has the distinction of being one of the last in the country to have integrated high school proms. There were young people, students, leaders in their own right, who supported the integration of their proms. They petitioned the local government to make the change so they could enjoy the company of all their peers during the special occasion of their prom.

An article in *Business Insider* in 2013 states, "In 2002, Taylor County High School near Columbus, Georgia, threw its first integrated prom that was featured on *CNN* and *Good Morning America* (though the following year, White students reverted back to a Whites-only prom)."

This is the racial climate I was born into back in 1952. This is my reality. As I drive through that same area today, I see the beautiful homes built far back into the distance, and I know that at one time the area was much, much different. The waterfall, the bridge, and the Coca Cola building remain, and when I see these things I am overwhelmed by a sense of nostalgia. I show these things to my grandchildren to give them a sense of family history. I point out what was once standing in this or the other place and try to give them a sense of being connected to the place where I, and my family members long before me, worked under difficult conditions but still found a way to enjoy ourselves in the lives that we lived. The memories invoked will be with me forever.

https://www.businessinsider.com/georgia-students-plan-interracial-prom-2013-4

My life story is obviously still unfolding. Being a recent retiree, I find I have time to pause and reflect on the numerous joys, sorrows, loves, and laughs that have comprised my life thus far, and from this, the idea to write this book was born. I was so unsure about just how to recount my life, which has been filled with a wide range of highs and lows and contains such a rich tapestry of family experiences. I questioned whether I had what it took to meet the challenge of writing this book, but I had to proceed because I knew I wouldn't rest until these stories were told. I was filled with a deep sense of urgency to capture and chronicle these stories, as they represent a vital part of who I am and the legacy I wish to leave behind. I am compelled by an inner drive to share my experiences with others. I believe that by doing so, I will not only honor my own journey, but also provide a source of inspiration, hope, and connection for those who may be considering writing their own stories.

Introduction

I thought long and hard about how to begin to put my life onto these pages, especially since my life is woven so intricately into the strands of so many other lives. If you have been a part of my life in some way, if you are part of my family—a family which I hold so dear to my heart—be ye not surprised to find yourself lovingly embedded in the stories herein told about the life of "Yang Yang." How could I not include you when you have been there for most of my life? You are a part of me and therefore many of my stories are your stories, too.

As previously alluded to, I willingly confide in you that that I experienced significant doubts about the value of sharing these stories, and whether I possessed the necessary skill to narrate it with the vibrancy, color, and richness which I believe they hold. The fact that you are now reading this book speaks to how I resolved those questions, but humor me if you will, as I take you down the path into the depths of my mind as I considered writing this book.

There was so much self-doubt that it overwhelmed my thoughts and threatened to forever obscure my vision for this book. I questioned my own story, my own memories, and my own experiences. *Me, write a book?* I wondered whether I had what it took to tell my stories with the authenticity, passion, and impact they deserved. I was full of uncertainty; still, I refused to give up. I knew I wanted to write about my life experiences, and I was determined to do it. I struggled with just the right way to express myself, but I came to the conclusion that it was worth it to give it a try. Is it perfect? Perhaps not, but I have made peace with it.

I committed myself to writing like never before with the aim of immortalizing the stories of my life and leaving somewhat of a legacy for my family. I wanted them all to know the heart and soul of not only their predecessor, Dr. Mary Ann Gibson, but also of those who came before me—the Gibson line who struggled through adversity to achieve meaningful accomplishments that reflect the very essence of what it means to be human. My hope was and is that these stories will serve as a demonstration of the strength and determination that runs through the veins of the Gibson family. Mostly, I share these stories as a *gift* to my family and to all those who seek inspiration, humor, and hope in this increasingly difficult world. If these pages offer but a glimmer of those things to only a few people, I will count this project as a success.

Chapter One
Born During the Jim Crow Era

The small town where I was born (Reynolds) in Taylor County, Georgia, is also the birthplace of the Reverend Earl Little, father of Civil Rights leader Malcolm X. The Black citizens in our town were mostly sharecroppers, and mostly poor. Like many rural towns in the American South, the little corner of the world where I was born has its own history of poverty and racial injustice. As I look back on my youth, I can still see the cotton fields on the outskirts of town as their bolls wave in the gentle breeze. Sharecropper families had generations of history tied to the very land I walked on every day, standing in the shoes of my ancestors. The field work could be grueling, working the crops for a small portion of the harvest. Our calloused hands and our skin made even darker by the sun told the story of how we spent our days on the land.

The landscape changed with the seasons, giving us beautiful wildflowers in the spring. The fields as I recall them were bathed in dreamy, gorgeous golden and copper light during the summer months, and our family gatherings to celebrate my father's birthday on the Fourth of July will always be special to me.

Fall was usually a time of excitement because of the harvest, a time to gather the fruits of labor.

The winters of my youth brought quiet and calmness as the cotton fields were generally barren in anticipation of spring when the cycle would repeat.

Cotton fields, woods, dirt roads, the fun and adventures I shared with my siblings, and the love of my hardworking sharecropper parents—these are among my earliest, fondest memories.

There are some wonderful things about my childhood, about my life growing up in Reynolds, Georgia, that I would not trade for anything. I was born in 1952. During that time, Taylor County was just as one might imagine: dirt roads in the country with plenty of sunshine and wide-open space for an imaginative child such as I was to grow and to explore. My parents, along with many other families in our area during that time, were mostly sharecroppers. Racial segregation was the order of the day during my youth. It was a deeply ingrained norm, firmly rooted in the minds of Black people like the sprawling roots of a birch tree deep in the earth—an inescapable reality for Black people.

1952 marked a period in American history that was silhouetted by racial segregation. At that time, laws and social norms dictated that Black people and White people should be kept separate from one another. Unfortunately, this separation was not merely confined to public spaces or institutions—it permeated every aspect of our daily lives—but still, it was all I knew because I was born into these times. My siblings and I never knew life to be any other way until the segregation laws were upended by the Civil Rights Act of 1964, the Voting Rights Act of 1965, and the Fair Housing Rights Act of 1968. The practical implications of segregation were no less than profound. We lived in separate neighborhoods from White people, we attended separate schools, and we even used separate public facilities. Public water fountains were marked "White Only" and "Colored."

We were fortunate in that the White people we knew were kind to us, but the world around us was starkly divided along Black and

White lines and I, like most other Black people, had to later learn to navigate this world with a sharp sense of caution and vigilance for the sake of our safety.

The story of my birth is in itself a reflection of a time when racism was rampant and pervasive, and when segregation was the norm. My mother, pregnant with me, made the bold decision to forgo the local hospital and instead chose a midwife to deliver me at home. Back then, midwifery was a common practice, especially among Black women who were often subjected to subpar medical care at the hands of doctors who were well-aligned with the dominant social positions on racial matters of the times. In those days, going to the hospital as a Black person was always a last resort, reserved only for emergencies when life or death hung in the balance. And even then, the experience was fraught with tension and discrimination. Black patients were relegated to a separate wing of the hospital, far away from the White patients, and often treated as second-class citizens by the doctors and nurses who provided the care. This is just how things were during those times.

It wasn't just the physical separation of Whites and Blacks that was so jarring; it was the deep sense of inferiority and dehumanization of Black people that accompanied it. Black people were not allowed to sit in waiting rooms with White people. The doctor's office waiting rooms were also segregated, and we were not afforded the same level of care and attention in these medical settings. We were made to feel like we didn't belong, like our lives were worth less than those of our White counterparts. I hesitate to visit doctors' offices to this day, and that hesitancy is rooted in the experiences of my family from my earliest memories surrounding medical care. My mother was wise to have all of her children safely in the comfort of her own home during those times.

In many ways, her decision to have a midwife attend to her during not just my birth, but the births of all her children, was an act of resistance, a refusal to be subjected to the indignities and injustices of the prevailing social order of the day. I count it as a small act of rebellion, but it spoke to a larger truth about the strength and resilience of Black people in the face of uneven odds. These problems, experienced by countless Black families all around the country, contributed to an overall sense of despair, hopelessness, and unrest. These conditions created the climate that fueled the Civil Rights Movement in the 1960s.

Being born during the era of Jim Crow, life had its major complexities for me and my family. Everyday life was rife with challenges, but my parents and grandparents never let hardships or challenges overshadow the happy moments. We never had much, but we were always grateful for whatever we did have. Whether it was sharing a meal together or simply enjoying each other's company, we found ways to create joy in our lives. One thing that was particularly special about our community was the sense of belonging. There were no strangers in our town; everyone knew each other, and we looked out for one another. It was common for neighbors to come over unannounced to share a meal, or to offer help whenever someone was in need.

My grandparents were a prime example of the values that were important to our community. They worked hard every day, both in the fields and in their home, yet they always found time to help others. They believed that no one should ever be left to struggle alone. It was a sentiment that was passed down to my parents, and to my siblings and me.

Despite the hardships, there were also moments of pure joy. My family would often gather in the evening, sitting around the table or on the front porch as the sun set, sharing stories and laughter. We would enjoy the sounds of nature, the crickets chirping and the fireflies dancing in the yard. It was a peaceful time, a time to simply be present with one another and to appreciate the beauty of life. Those moments of happiness reminded us of the peace and strength of our tight community and that even in the toughest times, there was always something for which we could be grateful.

Yes, there were some wonderful things about my childhood, about my life growing up in Reynolds, Georgia, that I would not trade for anything. Having one sister, Minnie, and three brothers, Chuck, Jimmy, and Jason, our playgrounds were the many unpaved dirt roads and open fields under the big, blue Georgia sky. As children, we didn't have many luxuries, but we had each other and a shared love for playing ball. Our favorite spot was a quiet street where cars rarely intruded, allowing us to play freely to our hearts' content.

We reveled in the freedom and safety of having a space to run, jump, and toss the ball around without fear of interruption or danger. However, as luck would have it, cars occasionally made their way down our beloved street. Instead of feeling annoyed or afraid, we saw it as an opportunity to start a new game. We all had our favorites, and each of us would lay claim to a certain car. Mine was, and remains to this day, the sleek and elegant Mercedes Benz. Whenever one of those beauties would roll by, I would feel a surge of pride as if it were really mine. *"That's my car!"* I would exclaim. The other kids would join in, shout my name, and affirm my ownership of the Mercedes. It was a silly game, but it brought us so much joy and added a new layer of fun to our already thrilling ball games. Even today, whenever I see a Mercedes Benz on the road, I can't help but smile and feel a sense of nostalgia for those carefree days of my childhood.

As a child, few things brought me as much excitement as seeing the massive big-rigs rolling down the road in our town. The sound of their engines roaring and the sight of their imposing size made my heart race as I stood in quiet reverence of these enormous trucks. They were wonders on wheels. I wasn't alone in this; all the kids in the area felt the same way, and we would gather eagerly whenever we heard the distant rumble of an approaching eighteen-wheeler.

We developed a special tradition when it came to these giants of the road. As the driver would pass by, we would bend our arms at the elbow, signaling for them to sound their horn. And, like clockwork, the driver would oblige, letting out a blast of sound that made us scream with wild excitement.

We would then race behind the truck, arms still bent, listening intently for the horn to sound again, trying to keep up with the truck until it was out of sight.

Sometimes, we were lucky enough to encounter something even more exciting—a convoy of military trucks. These were a rare sight, but when they came by, we could not contain our excitement. We would run alongside the trucks, waving our arms and cheering as the soldiers looked on with amusement. And every so often, to our immense delight, the soldiers would toss out military rations, and to us, they were like gifts from above.

As I look back on those days, I can't help but smile at the innocence and joy I experienced as a child. The simple pleasure of seeing a big-rig or a military truck passing by was enough to fill us all with wonder and excitement. Those memories will stay with me for a lifetime.

Chapter Two
Parents Meeting

My father often spoke fondly of his hometown of Macon, Georgia, but it was in Taylor County where he met the love of his life, my mother. She would often share the romantic story of how they met, and it never failed to bring a smile to her face. She described it as love at first sight, and from that moment on they were inseparable. She told us how they would steal kisses behind birch and oak trees and whisper sweet nothings to each other. Their love grew over time and eventually, they married and started a family. My mother and her sister married two brothers in a beautiful bond that brought both families together.

Having one sister and three brothers, our playgrounds were the many unpaved dirt roads and open fields under the big, blue Georgia sky. We absolutely loved where we lived out in the country. We spent countless hours in the sun playing dodgeball, hide and seek, jack stones, jump rope, and hopscotch. One of my brothers even taught me how to play marbles, a game in which most girls showed little interest.

I have many fond memories of growing up in a household filled with love and laughter. There was always a sense of warmth and security that came with being surrounded by siblings who loved each other and parents who loved us the best way they knew how. We had our share of battles but there was never any doubt that we all loved each other.

My aunt and uncle had two boys, my cousins. We are a very athletic family and we spent countless hours together playing ball, going on adventures, and just enjoying each other's company. We were all so close that we considered ourselves siblings despite not sharing the same parents. Whenever we were at school and someone asked if we were related, we proudly told them that we were all brothers and sisters. It was our little fun secret, but it also helped us get free lunches at school, there being so many of us. Sadly my aunt and uncle and my cousins have all transitioned from this life. I miss them dearly and wish they were still with us, but I know that they are watching over us from heaven. My mother's brother, who I considered my favorite uncle, Uncle Robbie, has also transitioned from this earthly life. He was a kindhearted man who loved to help people in our community and beyond however he could. One of his passions was operating his heavy machinery, particularly his bulldozer. More about him and his bulldozer in a later story.

Chapter Three
Gib and Fiona

My parents are gone now, and I miss them every day. When I think about how life must have been for them as Black people growing up in the Southern part of the United States, I sometimes weep. I also feel a great sense of pride in their resilience and determination to survive. During the early twentieth century when the world as they knew it was changing all around them, my parents' relationship remained untouched by the outside forces surrounding them. The way in which my father lovingly addressed my mother with the nickname "Gal" was for us a demonstration of his affection for her.

Whenever he spoke of her he did so with great reverence and warmth, referring to her also as his "Old lady," a term of endearment that not only spoke volumes about the strength of their connection, but it also gave my siblings and me a sense of security that we could not understand at the time. As long as my mother was my father's "old lady," we knew we had nothing to worry about. To him, mother was the epitome of strength and grace, a woman who carried all the qualities that he so deeply admired. Their commitment to each other gave us a wonderful sense of security as children.

My mother responded to him with an equal measure of fondness, always lovingly calling him "Gib." She recognized his warmth and kindness and she felt blessed to have him in her life. It was clear to me that my parents' marriage bond was divine. They were perfect for each other. Their journey together through life was rife with fears, challenges, setbacks, uncertainties, but also with the determination to survive. They worked through difficult times to forge a path of safety and stability for themselves and for their children, a path that would allow us to navigate this difficult world that judged all of us chiefly by the color of our skin. Theirs was a very difficult job, but they were sustained by faith, love, and humor. Armed with those things, they endured and enjoyed more than fifty years together until my father transitioned from this earthly life. Catherine tried to convince my parents to renew their vows in a ceremony for their fiftieth anniversary, but it never happened. My mother would only agree on the condition that the ceremony be held in a big church, and my father couldn't be convinced of this idea.

On one especially happy and pleasant birthday, I received the most beautiful and extravagant bouquet of flowers anyone had ever seen. They were from my father. He insisted that the flowers be sent to me at the school where I worked. He knew that I didn't have a husband or any other man in my life to present such a gesture, and he stepped in to ensure that I knew I was loved. He worked in a recycling plant at the time, and part of his duties were to go around town collecting empty boxes from stores and schools. From time to time while he was in the schools, I think perhaps he saw some of the bouquets that some of the teachers had received from their husbands or significant others, and he wanted me to have the same experience. My bouquet was purple and gold and again, it was the loveliest I had ever seen.

Two days later, I got off work and went to the local hair salon, Open Beauty. It was a Friday afternoon, one that I don't think I will ever forget. The phone rang at the salon and Gregory, the beautician, answered. He hung up the phone, turned to me, and said calmly, "Go to the hospital. Your family is waiting for you. They didn't say why." As you can imagine, at that point, I was frightened, and my heart started racing. So much so that I could not force myself to go to the hospital. I was too scared. I just wasn't able to face whatever this bad news was, and I felt safer just going home. This was before the proliferation of mobile phones.

When I got home, my neighbors met me in the driveway with the news, saying, "Gib, your father died in the hospital or on the way there!" Hearing this, my legs became extremely weak. I felt as if I had been dealt a physical blow to my upper body, as if the wind had been knocked out of me. My neighbors continued talking to me, but I could no longer hear them. The news of my father's sudden death came as a devastating shock to me, and I was unable to cope. Once I caught my breath I let out a loud, gut-wrenching scream. My father was gone. It continues to hurt, but I feel grateful to have been a part of my parents' journey. I know that their love will continue to live on through their children and grandchildren for generations to come.

Chapter Four
Sang it, Fiona!

My siblings and I were fortunate enough to witness firsthand the power of love between our parents. This took many forms, but it was evident in one particular aspect of our parents' marriage, and that was my father's reaction to my mother's singing. To this day, we fondly recall the many instances when our mother would break out into song, and Daddy would proclaim loudly and proudly, *"My Fiona KNOW she can sang! Sang it, Fiona!"* Her voice was far from perfect, but it was filled with heart and soul, and it never failed to put a smile on Daddy's face, or a grimace on ours.

In fact, we thought Daddy couldn't possibly be hearing the same things we heard when Mama sang. We wondered if he was living in a parallel universe where the sounds coming out of Mother's mouth were actually music to his ears. Had Daddy lost his mind? What was happening? I really didn't know. Maybe it was one of those "Y'all don't know nothin' 'bout that" kind of things, which he said to us frequently.

My father's actual encouragement of Mother's singing, despite her lack of vocal talent, made us cringe just as much as Mother's singing itself did. And yet, he persisted. He would urge her to sing, pushing her to new heights of vocal terrorism while we shuddered and wished it would stop. Mother was so bold and confident when she sang that sometimes she would put her hands on her hips, lean backward a bit, and unleash her brand of singing that only my father could love. As a child, I was bewildered by this strangeness of my mother's voice. She could never be considered a good singer, but my father loved it. He would often make all of us sing along as well, while he hyped my mother up, admiring her voice. We would just laugh. It wasn't until I grew older and observed my father's reactions to her singing that I began to understand. Despite the off-key singing that filled the room, my father's gentle face remained serene and happy. His love-struck mannerisms around my mother and his admiration for her never waned, and his love for her would never diminish. It was then that I realized that my father wasn't deaf to the cringe tones of my mother's singing voice, nor was he being polite to her or living in a parallel universe where up was down and down was up. He simply loved my mother. He loved every part of her, even the parts of her that made her think she could sing. Through that observation I gained a newfound respect for the power of love. I realized that true love isn't about perfection or idealized expectations of one's partner in any way; it's about loving someone for who they are, warts and all. My father's love for my mother showed us that sometimes, the most beautiful things in life are the imperfect ones. We fondly remember our dear mother through those and other moments of joy and laughter. We will always treasure these memories, and the greater message they offer to us about the importance of cherishing the simple pleasures in life. My father seemed to have always understood this.

It's quite amusing to ponder how, as a child, I never fully grasped the significance of the moments I was living and the implications they would have later on in my life. Little did I know that those seemingly ordinary occurrences would eventually transform into cherished memories that would accompany me throughout my entire life.

In the midst of our daily routines, I was blissfully unaware of the impact my parents were making on my life. Their love and dedication were constant companions, always present but often taken for granted. I would wake up each day, and there they were, by my side, providing guidance, support, and unconditional affection. It never occurred to me that these simple acts of parental devotion would become the foundation upon which my sense of self and my values would be built.

Their presence was a reassuring constant, like the gentle embrace of a warm blanket. I would go about my day, engaged in play, learning, and exploration, blissfully unaware of the invaluable life lessons they were imparting in their own subtle ways. All of these moments contributed to shaping my character and instilling within me a sense of resilience, compassion, and integrity.

Looking back now, I realize that it was their consistent presence and unwavering love that nurtured my growth and provided a sturdy foundation for me to navigate the complexities of life. With their wisdom and foresight, they created an environment where I could flourish, unburdened by the weight of the future, and fully immersed in the joy and wonder of the present. In other words, they allowed me and my siblings to be children.

As the years passed and I embarked on my own journey into adulthood, I began to recognize the profound impact my parents had on shaping the person I had become. Their support and belief in me fueled my ambitions, and their lessons on persistence fortified my spirit during many times of adversity in my life. The memories we created together, often taken for granted in the innocence of youth, have transformed into treasures that I hold dear, and serve as a constant reminder of their love and the immeasurable influence they had on the trajectory of my life.

It is a remarkable realization to understand that the everyday moments spent with my parents, seemingly insignificant at the time, have evolved into lifelong memories that continue to shape my perspective and define the very essence of who I am today.

Chapter Five
Boundaries and a Sense of Peace and Harmony

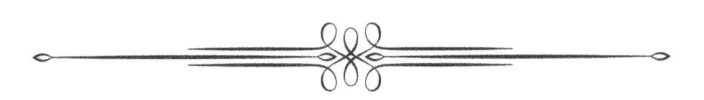

It was wonderful to grow up in a household with parents who maintained a sense of peace and harmony. The atmosphere was usually calm outside the typical boisterousness of five children, and any tensions that arose were quickly diffused with a sense of grace, respect, and an occasional, "A hard head makes a soft behind!"

Despite the inevitable struggles that all families encounter, my parents never allowed their disagreements to spill over into the realm of their children's awareness. As a result of their devotion to our well-being, I was spared the trauma and anxiety that can sometimes result from witnessing arguments and conflict between one's parents. They were also sure to never let us see or feel a sense of lacking or inferiority with regard to material things which were always in short supply. They provided everything we needed, and we had each other. We had no knowledge about the fact that our parents were only a generation or so out of slavery. They were proud and dignified, and their work as sharecroppers, oftentimes with us working the fields right beside them, never diminished their sense of worth as children of God.

We were fortunate that their approach to parenting was rooted in a deep understanding of the need for children to feel secure and protected. They knew that providing us with a sense of stability and tranquility was paramount to our development and well-being. Their commitment to shielding us from the harsh realities of life, to let us enjoy our childhood without the burden of adult concerns, was a testament to their love and devotion to our family.

Their insistence on maintaining boundaries between themselves and their children was not meant to exclude us or make us feel unimportant. Rather, it was a sign of their respect for us as individuals, with unique needs and perspectives that deserved to be acknowledged and protected. They knew that our presence in the room during their conversations could inadvertently cause us anxiety, fear, and/or confusion, and they chose to spare us that discomfort.

Reflecting on my upbringing, I am grateful for the wisdom and compassion of my parents, and how they created an environment where we could flourish and grow. Their bond and their commitment to providing us with a sense of security and stability allowed us to focus on the joys of childhood, unencumbered by the weight of adult worries.

Indeed, my parents' approach to parenting, with its emphasis on peace, harmony, and respect, including the occasional whipping when they felt it was necessary, has left its impression on me. I am forever grateful for the love and guidance they provided and the lifelong memories we all created together. Their example has inspired me to cultivate a similar sense of calm and tranquility in my own life and relationships, and for that, I am truly thankful to them.

Chapter Six
Dancing, Togetherness, and a Pig

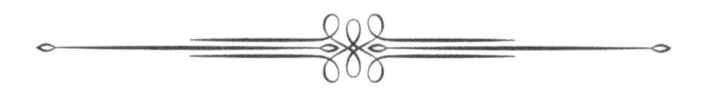

Call me biased, but my parents were truly an extraordinary couple. They were sharecroppers, hard working, and they loved each other. They were not perfect people by any stretch of the imagination, but they were warm, wonderful people, and their love was unbreakable. They were inseparable. Their devotion to each other left an impression on everyone who knew them. It wasn't just the longevity of their marriage that was remarkable, it was the way they treated each other every single day of their lives. Even after more than fifty years together, my parents would still hold hands while walking, kiss each other on the cheek, and laugh at each other's jokes as if they had just met.

They would spend hours talking about everything and nothing, enjoying each other's company in a way that seemed effortless. They simply enjoyed each other's company. There are so many moments from my childhood where I found my parents laughing together, completely in sync with one another. When they had disagreements, they always managed to talk it out and find a solution that worked for both of them. For the most part, my mother was a mild-mannered woman. I admired her ability to keep her cool and how she could handle any situation with grace and dignity. She never gave up on my father, even when things got tough. I know he felt the same way about her.

Growing up on a farm, my parents were very resourceful and made the most of what they had. They instilled in us the importance of hard work and self-sufficiency. Our family time often revolved around activities like fishing and hunting, which not only provided us with food but also served as valuable bonding experiences. My mother was an excellent cook. She would take the fish we caught and turn them into mouth-watering dishes. We would all pitch in and help with the cleaning and preparation, which made the meal even more satisfying because we all played a small part in bringing it to the table.

One of my fondest memories growing up was when Daddy would come home from his excursions in the woods. He always managed to come home with something special for us. My absolute favorite was when he would come home with apples, plums, and other delicious fruits that he had rolled up in his shirt. I can still remember the sight of him walking up the dirt road to our house, his shirt bulging with the bounty of the woods. As soon as he walked in the door, we would all gather around him, eagerly awaiting the treats that he had brought for us to enjoy. He would carefully unwrap the fruits, revealing their colorful skins and sweet, fragrant aromas while our mouths watered in anticipation.

As we enjoyed the fruits, he would tell us stories about his adventures in the woods. He would describe the animals and plants he had seen, and we would listen with unabated attention. Sometimes he would even bring back a little souvenir, like a feather or a small rock that played some part in his adventure through the woods.

Looking back, I realize that those moments with my father were more than just treats and stories. They were bonding experiences. They were also a reminder of the beauty and abundance that can be found in nature, and yet another reminder of the importance of appreciating the simple things in life.

My father's hunting skills were unmatched, and he always managed to bring home enough rabbits to feed the entire family and even have some left over to sell. His success as a hunter not only kept us fed but also provided some extra income.

In addition to fishing and hunting, we also had a bountiful garden that my parents tended to with great care. My siblings and I were responsible for planting and for helping to maintain the garden, and for dropping seeds for butter beans and other vegetables. It was hard work, but it was worth it. We had fresh vegetables all year round, and we rarely had to worry about going to the store to buy them. For us, life was full and always busy. Days were rarely, if ever, wasted as there was always something that needed to be done.

My parents' resourcefulness and dedication to providing for our family have left a lasting impression on me. They taught me that with hard work and determination, almost anything is possible. And as I sit down to enjoy a meal of freshly caught fish and home-grown vegetables, I am reminded of the valuable lessons they taught us. My father raised a pig, but it was not just any ordinary pig; he was a special pig. Daddy spent countless hours tending to him, making sure he had plenty of food, water, and a comfortable place to sleep. As the pig grew bigger and bigger, my father knew that he would eventually need to be slaughtered and processed. One cold winter morning, he put on his overalls and got his shotgun. He went outside to the pig pen, said a prayer, and shot the pig. It was a difficult task, but he knew it was necessary. He began the procedure of cleaning and processing the pig, making sure to use every part of the animal.

After a few weeks, the meat was finally cured and ready to be eaten. My mother fried up some of the country ham for breakfast, and the smell wafted throughout the entire house, waking up everyone with its mouth-watering aroma. The taste was even better than the smell; it was salty, savory, and had just the right amount of smokiness.

The country ham became a staple in our household. My mother would use it in her collard greens, green beans, and even in her cornbread. Years later, when I moved away from home, I found myself longing for the taste of my father's country ham. I would try to recreate it myself, but it was never quite the same. There was something special about the way my father raised and processed his pig that made the meat so amazingly delicious and unforgettable.

My father loved to dance. It was not only a hobby for him, but it was also a way for him to express his joy and love for life. He would often bring us children in on the fun, teaching us some simple steps and twirls, and we would all dance together in the living room or outside on the porch. I think that's one of the things I miss the most about him—his ability to bring people together and create moments of pure happiness through the simple act of dancing. It didn't matter where we were or what we were doing, when my father felt the rhythm of the music, he would begin to tap his foot, nod his head, and then suddenly jump up and start to dance. Sometimes it was while we were sitting around the dinner table, other times it was at a family gathering, and occasionally it was even in the middle of the grocery store aisle. His joy was infectious, and soon everyone around him would be clapping their hands, tapping their feet, and joining in on an impromptu dance party.

My mother was always a bit more reserved, but when my father grabbed her by the hand and pulled her up to dance, I could see the twinkle in her eye and the hint of a smile on her lips. I watched them one particular time and as they swayed together, it was clear that nothing else in the world mattered at that moment.

Even as I grew older, and my siblings and I would bring friends over to the house, my father never hesitated to break out in dance. His spirit was ageless and his love for music was extremely contagious. I'll always remember those moments when my father would suddenly feel the music in his soul and grab my mother's hand and pull her to her feet for a dance. It is a cherished memory that will live forever in my heart. They were an example of what true love looks like, and I feel so lucky to have had them as my parents.

Chapter Seven
A Child of Sharecroppers

My mother was raised mostly by her grandparents who seemed to worship husbands in general far beyond any normal, usual measure. Husbands could do no wrong. When I was a little girl, I watched my mother toil in the fields right alongside my father, doing every bit as much work as he did. She slogged hard every day under sometimes brutal conditions. In addition to the back-breaking work she did in the field every day, she also worked hard to maintain the home, with little to no help from my father. After working in the fields, he would come home and bathe, then he would relax. Mama, on the other hand, came in from the fields, bathed, and then began work again around the house: cooking, cleaning, and ironing. Field work was difficult, but there she was out there every day pulling every bit of her weight. Even as a child I knew she was exhausted from her day's work in the field, but her workday was not yet done once she arrived back home. My father's was though. This was simply his privilege for being a man. As a young girl I observed this imbalance and thought, "I'm never getting married if it means doing all that hard work!"

As children we pumped well-water, which we thought was the best water ever. On many occasions my siblings and I worked in the fields right alongside my parents. My dear father, who was born in Macon in 1924, lived in the South for his entire life. He was a gentle, sweet man, much like his own father. As a sign of the times in which he was born, words like "yessom" and "nosom" remained a part of his vocabulary until the day he died. My mother, who recently transitioned from this earth, also used this language. She believed, as my father did in his day, that it showed respect, a value, if you will, that was impressed upon her in her youth. In addition to his work as a sharecropper, as things were beginning to change, my father also worked as a foreman in a factory. He retired from Georgia Kraft where he earned a good living and provided well for us. We were fortunate. We never felt that we were deprived of anything. He took care of us, and this was not bad for a man who could neither read nor write. When he did finally learn to write his name, he always wrote it with pride.

During my childhood, before we had a washer and a dryer, we used barrels to catch rainwater for our washing. Each of us would go down the hill with our buckets to get spring water to bring home. We used a washboard to wash our clothes and we wrung them by hand. We then hung them on a clothesline to dry. My siblings and I worked when we were children. Working in the chicken house, it was our job to wash the eggs, let them dry, and then to grade them. I would often accompany my parents to the chicken coop to collect fresh eggs, but there was always a sense of apprehension that would grip me as we entered the coop, and I am afraid of birds to this day. The chickens would cluck and flap their wings, creating a noisy commotion that always made me extremely nervous. I was always uneasy about approaching the chickens, not knowing if they were in a good mood or if they would chase me and peck the hell out of me.

And then there were the times when the chickens would still be sitting on the eggs, which made the task even more daunting. We did this work mostly on the weekends and I felt a sense of dread as I approached those broody hens, trying to grab the eggs without causing any distress to the birds. The fear of being pecked was very real, and it added to my overall anxiety about doing this work. My fear notwithstanding, I understood the importance of egg duty. It was part of my job. We collected the eggs, counted them, and placed them in baskets before taking them to the next building, where they were washed, dried, graded, packaged, and put into crates. My uncles would take the eggs to the stores to be sold. Although we were children, we could do this work independently, even when the grown-ups were away doing other jobs. Another frightening aspect of the job was that occasionally we would have to catch the chickens by the legs and hold them upside down while the bosses gave them a pill, an injection, or clipped their wings. I never understood the purpose of this, but it was not a pleasant job by any stretch of the imagination. The chickens were young, and they would squirm around and peck at us, and we were always glad when the job was done so we could let the birds go. Let me tell you, I dreaded that work. Let me also tell you that to this day, I will not drive with my top down, because I'm still afraid of birds!

Chapter Eight
Mr. Oliver and a Nightmare

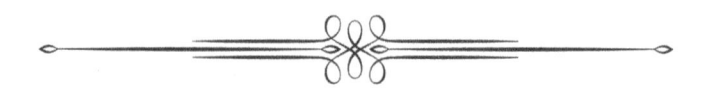

As children of sharecroppers, we worked hard, but we also played hard. We had plenty of sunshine, good food to eat, work to do, and the innocence of youth. I was also lucky to have a creative imagination on my side. I always knew that I wanted to be a teacher. When we played school outside under the Georgia sun, I was always the teacher. I had to be the teacher. If some other child insisted on being the teacher, then the game was over. If I couldn't be the teacher, then I refused to play. It was just as simple as that, like it or not!

When I was in school, I had a bus driver, Mr. Oliver. Mr. Oliver wouldn't let you get on his bus without saying "Good morning" or "Good afternoon." He would tell us, "You didn't stay at my house last night. When you see someone in the morning, you say 'good morning.' It's just the right thing to do!" I carried Mr. Oliver's moral lesson into my adulthood. When Mr. Oliver spoke, people listened. He had a booming voice that seemed to shake the ground beneath our feet. He also used to tell us fantastical stories, and one in particular, I know I will never forget. When he told a story, it was as if you were right there with him, experiencing every moment as if it were your own.

One particular story that always stood out was the one about the cow. We all sat in rapt, unabated attention as he described how the cow had been causing trouble on his property, destroying fences and eating crops. He had tried everything to get her to leave, but nothing worked. Finally, in frustration, he hit the cow with his fist so hard that she fell down dead. The way he described the scene, with the cow collapsing in a heap and Mr. Oliver standing over her, triumphant, was enough to make us all shiver. The imagery he created with that story was unforgettable. He never had any trouble with any of us kids on his bus. We were afraid of Mr. Oliver.

Despite his intimidating demeanor, Mr. Oliver was never unkind to us kids. In fact, he seemed to have a soft spot for us, and would often take the time to chat with us and share stories of his own childhood. But we never forgot that he was a force to be reckoned with, and the memory of that story about the cow lingered with us long after we had grown up.

In the midst of my fond memories of the joy and happiness that defined my childhood, there sits one memory of a not-so-pleasant experience. In fact, it was quite traumatizing. Memories of childhood are supposed to be joyful, carefree, and full of laughter. But for me, there is a fear that lingers to this day, an unresolved fear that I have carried with me into adulthood. I call it my "last-day-of-school phobia." Over the years, I have tried to suppress this fear, to rationalize my way around it, but it's always there, lurking in the shadows, waiting to resurface at any moment. And when it does, it brings with it a flood of anxiety and memories that are hard to shake.

I trace it back to the last day of school when I was in first grade. The sun was shining, and the air was filled with the excitement of the beginning of summer. The school bell had rung for the final time of my first-grade year, and all that remained was the bus ride home. We piled onto the bus, brimming with joy and excitement that freedom from school brings to children each summer. It was a celebration. "No more school, no more books, no more teacher's dirty looks," we chanted in unison. But then out of nowhere, the whole world turned upside down. The bus began to roll, and we were all thrown about like rag dolls. Suddenly, the bus crashed and landed bottom-side up. The bus began to take on water with the front-end upside down and completely immersed. The happy sounds of just a few moments before were replaced by blood-curdling screams of panic, terror, and pain. We were all trapped, helpless, and scared beyond our wildest imaginations.

Everyone ran and crawled to the back of the bus. The horrific cries and whimpers continued. We were trapped inside the mangled steel that had once been a school bus. Thankfully during that time, all K–12 students in our community rode the same bus. It was one of the older kids from the higher grades who had the presence of mind to kick out a back window so that we could begin to extricate ourselves.

It felt like an eternity before we were finally cut free, and even then, the cries and the panic continued. Once we were all free, my sister Minnie found a tree and held on to it for dear life. She would not let go of the tree. When the police arrived, they found her with her arms around the tree and asked if she was all right. The officer also asked her if the driver had been speeding. Between cries and whimpers, Minnie managed to answer the officer and said, "Yes, he was speeding. He was going twenty-five miles an hour!" She had no idea what constituted speeding, but I think her insistence in decrying "twenty-five miles an hour" and the other children chiming in to agree with her may have been the only thing that prevented the bus driver from getting into major trouble over the accident.

In the chaotic aftermath of the accident when emotions ran high and the air was wrought with tension, Minnie's simple words, mumbled through tears and fear, took on an unexpected authority. The other children, sensing the weight of the moment, agreed with Minnie and lent support to her claim.

At her young age, she definitely lacked a definitive understanding of what it truly meant to exceed the speed limit, but her firm conviction in pointing out what she thought was the high number of "twenty-five miles an hour" resonated with an innocence and honesty that was hard to ignore.

It was as if time momentarily stood still, as everyone processed the revelation. The bus driver's eyes widened, a mixture of guilt and relief washing over his face. I think he realized the potential consequences he could have faced had it not been for the unintentional testimony of Minnie and the other children. Their collective insistence on the speed of "twenty-five miles an hour" became a shield of protection for the bus driver. The principal came out to the accident site accompanied by some teachers from the school. It was all very traumatic, but outside of the two or three children that were taken to the hospital, we never received medical treatment or counseling, or any kind of psychological support. In the end it seemed that not too many people really cared about what happened to us.

The accident left me with a deep sense of fear, a fear that took root in my subconscious and manifested itself in the form of an irrational fear of travel. For many years, I avoided traveling as much as possible. The mere thought of getting on a plane, train, or bus was enough to send shivers down my spine. The fear was real, and it was paralyzing. I may have missed out on opportunities and experiences over the years due to my reluctance to travel, but I refused to let "what ifs" take up space in my mind forever. I tried to rationalize my fear, but deep down, I knew that it was rooted in the trauma of that bus accident. Every time I boarded a bus, the memories flooded back. The sound of the engine, the feel and sound of the wheels on the road, and the movement of the vehicle all brought me back to that fateful day.

As I got older, I tried to confront my fear head-on. I took baby steps, like short road trips with friends or family, and eventually worked my way up to longer journeys. It wasn't easy, but I refused to let my fear control me. I wanted to experience all that life had to offer, and I knew that my fear of travel was holding me back. The memories of that bus accident still haunt me, but I refuse to allow it to completely paralyze me forever. I have learned to cope with my fear if only to a small degree, to acknowledge it and face it head-on. And while I may never fully overcome it, I am determined to not let it hold me back from the experiences that life has to offer. That day changed me forever. It taught me that life can be unpredictable, and that even the most joyful moments can be shattered in an instant. I learned further how important it is to appreciate the precious moments of life and to never take anything for granted.

Chapter Nine

The End of Segregation and a Troubling Graduation

The end of segregation was a pivotal moment in our lives, as it opened our eyes to things we never knew we never knew. Growing up, we were never really aware of our poverty. We started asking questions when we got older but as kids, we never knew. It was just normal for us to have an all-Black neighborhood, and to go to an all-Black school. It was only later that we began to think about our parents and grandparents and their closeness to chattel slavery in Georgia. Our parents provided for our needs, and we were never lonely or lacked ideas for adventures because we had each other to play with outside, basking in the warm sun and digging our hands into the rich soil. Our greasy lunch bags never bothered us until we saw other kids with "proper" lunch pails. My mother reminded us to bring those bags back home so we could use them again for the next day's lunch. Suddenly, we felt ashamed and embarrassed to be seen with such things. My father would try to make us feel better by telling us that the other kids envied what we had in our bags.

Despite our lack of material possessions, we were rich in spirit. We encouraged each other in sports, cheering on our teammates and congratulating everyone at the end of every game or race. The

White kids missed out and they knew it. They envied us. We played for the love of the game, without the pressure and ugliness that competition can sometimes bring. However, after segregation ended, the coaching mandates changed, and winning became the sole focus. It was no longer about doing your best; it was suddenly about leaving your opponents in the dust and crushing them. It was then that we realized our innocence was beginning to fade.

My father worked hard chopping wood for the fire that kept us warm. It wasn't until later that I realized one could actually buy wood. It was a surprise to learn that there were things we didn't know about the world beyond our small community. Growing up in the segregated South, our world was limited to our own neighborhood. We never went to White people's houses, and so we had no idea of the finery and luxuries they enjoyed. It was not until later in life that we discovered that they had indoor bathrooms, a concept that was completely foreign to us. We, like most Black families, had an outside toilet known as an outhouse.

Using an outhouse was a daily occurrence for us, and we never thought twice about it. It was just a part of life for us. We would go out in the cold, in the rain, or in the dead heat of summer to use the outhouse, whatever the weather may have been. It was not always a pleasant experience as one can imagine. In the winter, the outhouse would be freezing cold, and in the summer, it was hot and humid. We had to contend with the many bugs, flies, and other critters that would often take refuge inside. We accepted our circumstances because we knew no better. It was not until we began to interact with White people that we realized the vast differences in our living conditions. It was a shock to learn that they had indoor bathrooms with running water, and that they did not have to brave the elements each and every time they needed to use the toilet.

I was surrounded by poverty and the struggles of sharecroppers who made up the majority of the Black community. The town, like many rural areas in the South, had a history of racial inequality that

I was largely unaware of at the time. It wasn't until much later, when segregation had ended and I had grown older, that I began to fully grasp the extent of the challenges faced by my parents and other Black American families during those times.

As I reflect on my childhood in Reynolds, Georgia, the small town where I was born, I realize that it was a place where the harsh realities of racial segregation and poverty were ever-present. Looking back through history books and newspaper headlines, it is clear that the early 1950s in the American South were plagued by real problems, and while there was much that we were unaware of due to our age and our parent's protection, my hometown was no exception.

Despite all the hardships, my parents saw to it that my childhood had its distinct moments of innocence and joy. However, I cannot help but wonder how different my life may have been if I had been born in a different time and place, where my skin color was not a barrier to opportunity and equality, and where my skin color never held a risk over my life. Nonetheless, my experiences have shaped me into the person I am today and have given me a greater appreciation for the advancement of our society as the fight for change continues. The horrific lynchings of Black people in the South and elsewhere, and the fear they induced, along with the unrest that was brewing like a volcano on the brink of eruption, were major factors that contributed to the end of the freedom and pleasure we enjoyed in childhood.

We worked hard to not allow ourselves to be defined by our hardship and the intense racial climate of the day. We were very proud of our community, and more importantly, we had a strong sense of family closeness and togetherness. We looked out for each other and supported one another, and that was what mattered to us the most. It was not until the end of segregation that we were able to fully integrate into society and experience the same opportunities and privileges as our White counterparts, and how I would later become a teacher.

There were some wonderful things about my childhood, about my life growing up in Reynolds, Georgia, that I would not trade for anything because despite the oppressive weight of segregation, my family and I persevered. We found joy and solace in our community, in our resilience, and in our traditions of celebrating one another that continues to this day.

Graduation

Although we had moved to Roberta, my daily routine remained the same: attending school in Taylor County. It was in this county that my daughter Catherine came into the world, a significant event that coincided with my eleventh-grade year. However, Taylor County carried a heavy burden from its history as the last to integrate. The atmosphere was tense, marked by frequent riots and protests that seemed to unfold daily. The White students, it seemed, had no desire to coexist with us. They vehemently resisted the idea of sharing their educational institutions with us, refusing to accept our presence. But what they failed to grasp was that we, too, would have preferred to remain within the confines of our own community. Integration was forced upon us as well, and we were content with our own people and our own way of life. In our community, there was no notion of inferiority, no cutthroat competition. Instead, we embraced a profound sense of belonging, love, and togetherness. It was a place where we felt safe and secure, shielded from the uncertainties and otherness that we were now made to confront. So why should we be expected to relinquish this cherished haven for the sake of a strange and foreign new reality that was thrust upon us?

Amid the storm of unrest and division, amid the strained relationships and racial tensions, I somehow managed to forge a connection with one or two White classmates. Among them was Valerie, a girl whose tears summoned me near the eve of our graduation night.

As I saw her in distress, her face etched with anguish, my heart reached out to her, eager to alleviate her pain. I couldn't help but inquire, wanting to understand the source of her profound sorrow, "What's wrong?" My voice was laced with genuine concern.

Valerie, overcome by her emotions, poured out her heart to me, expressing a deep-seated remorse. She felt an overwhelming sense of guilt, the weight of a burden that she struggled to bear. "I just feel terrible," she whispered, her voice trembling with regret. In my attempts to bring solace, I sought to uplift her spirits, pointing out the impending joy of our graduation. "We're about to embark on a new chapter in our lives, Valerie. This should be a time of celebration," I suggested, hoping to infuse some optimism into her troubled soul.

But her response, laden with a profound sadness, shattered my attempt to comfort her. "You don't understand, Mary Ann. You just don't understand," she lamented, her voice tinged with a mixture of frustration and despair. Realizing the gravity of her distress, I fell silent, vowing to be a patient listener, granting her the space she needed to unburden herself. And then, after moments that felt like an eternity, Valerie gathered herself, her sobs subsided, and she began to reveal the truth that had shaken her to her core.

She disclosed a secret that seared through the facade of unity we were meant to embrace on graduation night. The White students, those who had walked the hallowed halls alongside us, had already held their own private commencement ceremony—a clandestine affair that excluded us, their Black peers. The forthcoming graduation, the one we had eagerly anticipated, was but a mere charade, a hollow spectacle bereft of authenticity. For all intents and purposes, the White students had already bid farewell to their high school years, leaving us, their Black counterparts, dishearteningly cast aside.

Valerie and others suggested that we not go to the graduation, that we should protest and just not show up. It was ironic that they would suggest that we refuse to go get something we earned, something which they had already received behind our backs. Their ceremony had already been held, and they already had their diplomas.

In that moment, the magnitude of the injustice, the cruel realization that we were deemed unworthy of sharing a stage with our peers, weighed heavily upon us. We were deprived of the collective and inclusive celebration, the acknowledgment of our accomplishments, and the public recognition that our hard work and dedication merited. It was a stark reminder of the deeply ingrained divisions that lingered, even in the realm of education.

As Valerie's revelation settled within me, I grappled with a mix of emotions: anger, disappointment, and a lingering sense of betrayal. Yet, amid the turmoil, a flicker of determination ignited within my being. I realized that the fight for equality, for a true integration of hearts and minds, was far from over. Our graduation, marred by exclusion, became a stark symbol of the barriers we still needed to dismantle, the prejudice we still needed to overcome. Valerie's discomfort was a testament to her own guilt. It now mirrored the collective pain we shared as we stood on the precipice of adulthood. And in that moment, I vowed to honor our struggles by forging a path toward a future where no one would be subjected to such indignity, where unity and acceptance would reign supreme.

Chapter Ten
Chuck, Jimmy, and the Irish Potato

My father was an expert marksman, fisherman, and hunter. He learned these valuable skills from his father, and in turn, taught them to his sons. My brothers became proficient, but it was Chuck who seemed to pick up these skills as if by instinct.

Chuck was a good-looking guy in his youth, and he still is. With beautiful light-green eyes and soft, loose hair, his children bear the same lovely features.

Aside from the basic and requisite education on gun safety my father taught them, Chuck just seemed to already know what to do, and he was raring to go. "Lemme have the gun, Daddy. I already know how to use it!"

"I know you think you already know everything, son. But you gon' be patient here until I'm comfortable that you know what you're doing with this here gun. This ain't fun and games you know, you could hurt yourself or somebody else, so you just quiet down and listen up." He understood Chuck's impatience, but gun safety was of utmost importance to him, and he wanted to prevent an accident.

My father set up tin cans in the backyard so he could first demonstrate, and then he allowed Chuck and my other brothers to practice. They spent long afternoons stacking and resetting those tin cans over and over again. Chuck stood out, though. He had an innate talent for marksmanship. Maybe because he seemed to have a greater interest than my other brothers who were not *uninterested*, it was just that they didn't show the same level of excitement for marksmanship that Chuck showed.

Chuck became so good that he could hit a fly's wings at a hundred yards. His skills were so impeccable that he could hit the center of his target blindfolded. His precision with the weapon was quite impressive. He didn't need months of training. He understood instinctively the workings of the machine, how to spot and line up his target, and how to fire successfully.

When he was a child, Chuck was always quiet, reserved, and introspective. He was not one to speak often but when he did, people generally paid attention. He would spend hours in quiet contemplation, working quietly on his wood crafts and fashioning useful gadgets and tools out of wood, stone, nails, or whatever other materials were available to him at the time. He always watched my father very closely, almost becoming his shadow. He paid close attention to everything my father did, and his own skills began to develop as a result of the attention he gave to every detail of what my father did with the shotgun. My father's job in this, which he executed masterfully, was to see to it that Chuck understood the inherent danger the weapon posed if ever used improperly.

Chuck's mild and quiet manner was not without a few pitfalls. His quiet and gentle nature seemed to provoke a measure of annoyance in the heart of his oldest brother Jimmy. "Why's he always so quiet? What's he all the time up to?" Chuck's quiet and still nature bothered Jimmy to the point of vexation. He took issue with his brother's ability to enjoy the simple pleasures of life. Chuck was just too quiet for Jimmy's liking. It was a characteristic in stark contrast to Jimmy's more boisterous, playful, and outgoing personality. "Leave me alone, Jimmy!" "Get away from me!" "Mama, will you make Jimmy leave me alone?" These were the frequent refrains from Chuck after Jimmy would push, shove, or otherwise annoy him.

Jimmy just wouldn't let up. He would take Chuck's tools or whatever Chuck happened to be working with and run off with them. Chuck would chase him and retrieve his property, but the victory was always short-lived. It wasn't long before Jimmy would be back again in true aggravating-big-brother fashion, pushing and shoving, and snatching objects away from Chuck and running away. Jimmy was a class-A pest to Chuck and no matter how many threats Chuck made, Jimmy remained committed to his role as a major pest in Chuck's life.

But then suddenly, Chuck stopped complaining and telling on Jimmy. He took up a new hobby instead. He stopped chasing Jimmy on the many occasions when Jimmy would snatch his things away from him and run. He stopped yelling for Jimmy to leave him alone as his pleas seemed only to spur Jimmy on anyway. Chuck became engrossed in his new hobby; a strange thing it was. He sat quietly, slowly filling an Irish potato with nails. "What a bizarre thing to do!" I thought.

Why would anyone put nails in an Irish potato? Chuck was wasting food, but I never told on him. I left him alone to mind his business and I minded mine. It seemed like every time I looked up, there was another nail driven into that potato. He kept going on and on and on, filling that potato with nails. What he intended to do with it was anybody's guess. As far as I was concerned, it was a silly thing to do, putting nails in a potato. But again, I left him to his business while I attended to mine.

Chuck had long since ceased complaining about Jimmy's bedevilment. He seemed to just accept his fate at the hands of his bothersome brother. He just sat quietly with his potato. Still, Jimmy showed no signs of letting up. Chuck was damned if he did, damned if he didn't. So he didn't. One day, Jimmy again observed Chuck in his quietness. He ran up to him and tapped him on the head for what must have seemed like the hundredth time for Chuck. Of course, Jimmy ran off again immediately after. Chuck simply and quietly recentered himself and didn't say a word.

Later that same day, Jimmy, who had become emboldened and accustomed to getting away with pestering his brother, showed up again for more of his hit-and-run shenanigans. He tapped Chuck on the head over and over again and then off he ran, again thinking he had gotten away with it as usual. This time however, Chuck sprang to action. He was an excellent outfielder. He could throw a man out at home base from center field. He had such a long arm that it was given its own nickname: "The Rifle."

Finally fed up with Jimmy's foolishness, Chuck quietly stood up and pitched his Irish potato full of nails after Jimmy, who had taken off running. If I had not seen this with my own eyes, I never would have believed it. As Jimmy turned the corner running full speed, Chuck's Irish potato bent and turned the corner to follow him and connected with the back of Jimmy's head. The damned potato turned the corner!

Once the potato made impact, it hung on for dear life. Jimmy, still running, screamed, "Maaaaa-ma, Maaaaa-ma!" as he ran toward the White people's house where our mother was working. We all took off after him.

That is, all of us except Chuck. He sat there as cool as the center seed of a cucumber, working on yet another Irish potato lest Jimmy try him again on another occasion.

We finally caught up to Jimmy, who was still running and screaming. "Hold still. Quit moving, stop screaming so we can get the potato out of your head, boy!" We ran after him as he was screaming and bleeding and somebody in the chase yelled, "You should've kept running straight, Jimmy. You shouldn't have turned the corner and the potato wouldn't have hit you!"

We had to catch him before he got to the house where our mother was working. If he had made it there to her job screaming and bleeding like that, it would have meant a whipping for all of us for acting up and embarrassing her. We pleaded with him not to tell on us. Jimmy knew beyond a doubt that it was Chuck who had inflicted that perfectly timed throw of the potato. No one else would have had such timing and accuracy in hitting his target.

Chuck's potato method of discouragement worked on Jimmy like a charm. Our parents didn't punish Chuck over the incident, and Chuck had no more problems out of Jimmy, even to this day. Jimmy was defeated, declaring, "Chuck is crazy. He don't play fair. He's crazy, he don't have good sense!"

Jimmy learned to leave Chuck alone because he thought he was crazy, but Chuck simply had and still has his own way about him, even though in many ways he was very much like my father.

Jimmy running and catching the Irish potato to the head reminds me of another time he sustained a head injury. It was a hot, humid Saturday afternoon when we left the house with our father to help him raze an old barn that had become an eyesore on his employer's property. It was near a chicken farm. Jimmy was excited to go because his friend, Tim, would be going with us to help work on the barn. It was an old barn used to store odds and ends like hay, old crates, boxes, and cartons. We had to cross a highway to get there so the only time we ever went there was when we were with my father.

We helped my father by methodically pulling out the old planks on his instructions. We had been working for quite some time in the hot sun, and we were making great progress. We could see straight through from the front to the back of the barn. After some time, my father said he was going to get us some refreshments, and that he wouldn't be away for long. He told us specifically which planks to be careful to avoid. He explained the danger of an uncontrolled collapse of the barn, and that certain planks needed to remain intact to prevent such an accident. Jimmy and Tim were standing at the back of the barn while I stood in front of the barn near my father. Soon after my father left, Tim pulled one of the forbidden planks. I could hear the creak and the crackle and screamed at the top of my voice, "It's gonna fall!" Tim stood back, but Jimmy ran forward. All he had to do was step one foot back, but I think my scream made him run toward me, which means he ran straight through the collapsing barn with the planks flying everywhere. I screamed in horror as I watched the planks come crashing down on him as he was running toward me at the front of the barn. At one point, we could no longer see Jimmy, and we knew he was hurt badly. I believe my father may have heard the collapse and saw the huge dust ball, and he came running back.

When he got to Jimmy, we could all see that he was really hurt. He had a head injury. My father lifted Jimmy's hair in the wounded area and the scalp came up as well. It was horrible and we were so afraid for our brother. We thought we had lost him, buried under the debris of the collapsed barn. My parents took Jimmy to the doctor. There were no broken bones, and his scalp injury would heal over time. He never really slowed down and was back to his old self in what seemed like no time. We count it a miracle that he survived.

And speaking more about Chuck, growing up, he was what one would call "rugged." For example, he was and still remains the silent type with impeccable survival skills. He, along with my other brothers, can tell you everything about hunting, fishing, gardening, and even how to remove a tick. Chuck enjoyed the old westerns and he always loved having a dog at his side. Once, he and I decided to buy a puppy together and become co-owners of the pet. We paid about ten or twenty dollars for the pup, but it was clear that Chuck was better suited to keep him than I was. The dog, who we named "Tiger," never listened to me about anything, but he obeyed Chuck's every word. Tiger protected Chuck, and even when Chuck got married, he kept Tiger with him.

We had a family dog at one time, and this dog was called "Red." My father, who never really liked dogs, seemed to really love Red. Red wasn't what you would call a nice dog, though. He was mean.

He bit nearly everyone in the neighborhood. Once, when Jimmy's middle son Kelly was young, he went outside, and soon after, we heard the child screaming. We ran out to find him on the ground, biting the dog. This makes me think about something Jimmy's son Bobby once did. He was out playing with one of his friends and we noticed that when he came into the house he had a dog's bowl in his hand. We asked him why he had the bowl, and he told us that he was just taking care of his dog. The thing was, he didn't even have a dog. We didn't think too much of it and we just let it go, but he kept running back and forth into the house for different things. We eventually looked out to see what he was doing. What we found was that he had his friend locked in the doghouse, with the poor kid screaming for somebody, anybody to let him out. I enjoyed spending time with my nephews, and my sister and I took delight in watching our children play together.

We had our front porch version of the popular television program called *The Gong Show*. If the judges deemed the talent good, then the performers could finish their performance. If the performance was deemed bad, the judges would hit the gong to immediately stop the performance. In our homemade version of this show, Minnie and I were the judges. Her middle son Doug would sing, "She'll Be Comin' Round the Mountain When She Comes," and his poor feelings were so hurt when we laughed and gave him the gong that he would cry. My son Andrew sang some song called "Hoochie Coo," and we wondered where the hell he got such a song.

Andrew's daughter, my granddaughter Andria, is a powerful spirit. Much like her father who she completely adores, she has a mind of her own. Andria is definitely a warrior, and she is a fiercely protective mother hen when it comes to her children, much like me. I am so pleased to say that my relationship with her grows stronger and stronger each day.

Tim is my oldest grandchild, and we share an incredibly strong bond together. However, my only regret is that I wasn't present in his life while he was growing up. Nevertheless, he has graciously forgiven me, and the most heartwarming moment was when he approached me to ask for forgiveness himself. God has given me a truly amazing grandson. Tim explained that he simply didn't know the full story and had relied on what others had said about me. However, through some divine intervention, his heart was touched. Instead of harboring any hatred that others might have expected him to have, he learned to respect and love me. He described me as a loving, kind, and caring person, and then he called me "Grandma." That day, I was overwhelmed with gratitude and felt deeply honored. With tears in my eyes, I humbly asked for his forgiveness, to which he responded, "Grandma, there's nothing to forgive." It was a truly heartfelt moment. I told him how much I love him, and we embraced tightly. Since that day, we have been inseparable, and nothing can come between our unbreakable bond. It's a love that will last forever. I love you, Tim, more than words can express.

I want to talk a bit about King, now. My nephew King is hilarious just like his father, Jimmy. As a child, King had great faith in God. When he was at my house and would sometimes fall and hurt himself, he would come in my room and ask me to pray for him. Later on he stopped asking and would get the oil and rub it on his bleeding knee and run back out the door and continue to play. Once we had a softball game but there weren't enough girls, so we would either have to cancel the game or get a little child to play with us. The other team agreed to this, and King was our catcher. We didn't want the other team to know just how good he was. We fooled them. When the game began, King almost hit a home run left-handed. The other team was upset and complained to the umpire, but it was too late; the umpire had already approved. He won the game for us that day. He has a kind and warm heart. He loves peace, and for everyone to have fun. He is my baby also.

Going down memory lane here, I am also reminded of how observant my sister Minnie's boy Solomon was. I used to take him to class with me from time to time when I was a student at Fort Valley State University. He was extremely observant and would tune in to every conversation he heard. On one occasion, I wanted to confide something to a friend, but because of Solomon's presence, I reconsidered and told my friend I would just tell her later.

Apparently, the wait would have been too much for Solomon, so he blurted out, "No, tell her now!" He was a sweet, nosy little something.

I had a class assignment once which required me to conduct and record an interview. With Solomon by my side, I took the opportunity to interview him. I asked whether he had any singing talent. Without a moment's hesitation, he broke out in song, boldly singing "I don't want no peanut butter and jelly." I thought this was a really good interview to present to my class, and I was sure that I would receive a good grade.

Soon after, Solomon expressed his desire to interview me in return. Eager to participate, I welcomed the opportunity, convinced that it would contribute to enhancing my grade even further. With a straight face, he posed to me a single question: "When do you plan on fixing your chipped tooth?" I didn't make any edits to the tape, and I presented it to my class as it was. Everyone, including the professor, was quite entertained. They thought the interviews were hilarious. Another thing about Solomon is that, to this day, he refuses to allow himself to be a passenger in a vehicle if his brother Doug is behind the wheel. It happened a long time ago when Solomon first began to distrust Doug's driving. Doug and Solomon are brothers, and Doug is the oldest. As a youngster, Doug loved to play, meddle, and have fun with everything he did.

When they were boys, their father bought Doug a motorbike and Doug loved it. He was exhilarated by the freedom and independence it brought him, the sound of the motor humming, and the high speed it could reach. He rode the bike whenever he could, sometimes all day. He also allowed his brother Solomon and his first cousin Andrew to have rides.

The motorbike would accommodate two riders at a time and on one occasion, Doug was at the helm and Solomon was the passenger seated behind him. Solomon held on for dear life. As they rode along, Doug hit a ditch, the impact of which sent Solomon flying through the air before he landed in a hard fall. Solomon cried out as he hit the ground, but Doug never turned around to go back and check on him to see if his brother was all right. He just kept going. Solomon walked home hurt and crying, and we tried to figure out what happened to him. Solomon never rode with him again, and still doesn't trust Doug's driving to this day.

Thinking of Doug, a wonderful person with a heart of gold who would do whatever he could for anyone, takes me back to the time when he was very young. He liked to refer to himself as "the baby." He wanted to play Telephone frequently. This was a game where, with a pretend telephone, he insisted that we hold a pretend receiver to our ears and say, "Who is it?" He would then reply with his favorite response, "It's Doug, Doug the baby."

He also had a wonderful sense of humor. When he younger, he was referred to as "Sideline Doug" by his football friends. He was called this because he never liked to be hit on the football field, and to prevent being hit, he would run out onto the sidelines.

Chapter Eleven
Jason, Castor Oil, and a Mean Neighbor

My brother Jason was born prematurely. He was so small and so fragile that my mother worried that she might lose him. As he began to grow, her fears remained, and she continued to exercise extreme caution with him. She was very protective of Jason, and we all thought he had it a bit easier than the rest of us. He did few, if any, chores around the house. My son Andrew was also born prematurely, and I took the same care and precaution with him that I saw my mother take with Jason. Once, as my father was leaving the house, he gave Jason a chore to do, telling him that the chore needed to be done before he returned home. Jason couldn't be bothered to do the chore. My father returned home only to find the chore undone. "Why didn't you do your chore, Jason? Didn't I tell you to have it done before I got back?" my father asked. Jason's reply was, "I just didn't feel like it." Without another word, my father walloped his behind, propelling him into the next room due to Jason's lanky frame.

Jason was so slender that the force of my father's swat to his behind sent him flying into the next room. My mother jumped up and intervened, telling my father, "Don't you ever hit my baby again!" I don't recall that he ever did. It's funny that now, Jason is taller and more stout than my other two brothers, Chuck and Jimmy.

I was an exceptionally precocious child, and I had a level of skepticism that made it impossible for anyone to tell me something and expect me to believe it offhand. My innate skepticism became apparent to my mother on those rare occasions when she would line up my siblings and me to administer our annual dose of castor oil, intended to safeguard us from winter colds.

In her effort to calm our apprehension about taking the castor oil, my mother assured us that there was nothing to worry about. She was confident in assuring us that it had no taste whatsoever, and that it would be an effortless and flavorless experience. However, my young discerning palate knew better. I was well aware of the repugnant taste of castor oil, and I was determined to avoid it at all costs. I protested, making it clear that I had no intention of subjecting myself to the wretched taste of that oil. I wanted no part of it. I would rather have a cold during the winter. "No, no, dear. It doesn't taste bad at all. In fact, it has no taste or smell whatsoever." She wasn't fooling me.

My poor sister Minnie attempted to display courage in the face of the challenge, and she valiantly tried to overcome the horrible taste only to find herself promptly regurgitating her dose. My brothers, on the other hand, seemed to have no qualms about ingesting the castor oil. They obediently swallowed the oil, and nonchalantly went about their business without any fuss or complaint. My mother was undeterred by my stubbornness, and she kept insisting that the oil was not only tasteless, but also odorless. "If I were blindfolded, I would still be able to smell it and taste it!" The sight of Minnie's unfortunate episodes of vomiting only served to reinforce my conviction that the oil was far from being tasteless and odorless. I remained resolute in my refusal.

From a young age, I recognized my inherent dislike for mean-spirited people, a sentiment that continues to resonate strongly within me even today. There is something about the essence of a person who harbors a cruel nature that unsettles me deeply, compelling me to steer clear of them whenever possible. This mean-spirited characteristic was epitomized by a particular woman who resided in our neighborhood during my formative years—a woman who exuded an aura of meanness. Her reputation as a mean lady was widely recognized and acknowledged by everyone in the community. Interacting with her was an exercise in discomfort and irritability because she had no inclination whatsoever toward pleasantry or kindness.

One fateful day, this lady's animosity was directed toward me, an innocent child. I did not cower, cry, or run away from her in fear, and neither did I allow her nastiness and her bitterness to slide by me. I knew for sure that a full reprimand from my parents would be imminent, but I didn't care. I felt an overwhelming sense of responsibility to confront her. If the burden of telling her what she needed to hear fell upon my young shoulders, it was no problem. I could bear the weight of it. In my bravest, most resolute voice I told her, "When you die, you're going to hell!"

The impact of my words left my mother mortified. She promptly prepared herself to reprimand me for my audacity. However, in that crucial moment, my hero, my father, intervened, stepping forward to protect me from the consequences of my boldness. "No, Fiona. The child merely said what everybody else in this neighborhood has wanted to say for years. Let the child be."

Chapter Twelve
Favorite Uncles

I was fortunate to have one of the best uncles ever, my Uncle Robbie. My mother and Uncle Robbie were siblings. When the other children were a bit too hard on me, Uncle Robbie was always there to protect me. He was kind, gentle, and sweet. He made time for me, he talked to me and he listened to me, he believed me whenever I told him something, and he gave me the greatest sense that I was important in this world. Now, if Uncle Robbie was my favorite uncle, Minnie had her favorite uncle too: our paternal Uncle Frank. She was also his favorite.

One day, Uncle Frank shared with me what he intended to sound like a hard and fast cemented rule. The rule was that whoever he walked around the house would take on his personality, and that that person would be sweet, just like him. Naturally, he walked Minnie around the house. So now, according to his rule, Minnie would be the sweet one among us. Being the precocious young person that I was, I responded to him, saying, "Hell, you ain't sweet." I felt it had to be said. I didn't care if my mouth got me in trouble or not. His words did sting a bit, and I cried. Of course, when I saw Uncle Robbie, I told him about it. Like the true hero he was to me, he picked me up and walked *me* around the house, telling me that *I* would be sweet like him, and he was indeed the sweetest. I felt so much better.

Like so many of us, Uncle Robbie was also a bit of a jokester. He had a large, beautiful pond on the back of his property. When I had grown older, I thought a brisk walk around the circumference of this huge pond would be a great way to get in some exercise. It wouldn't hurt to get in better shape, I thought. The first lap around the lake was pleasant enough. It felt really good to be out there in the fresh air and sunshine. I found the second lap a little more challenging, though. I had totally misjudged the size of the pond and my ability to make it around its circumference. In fact, my short legs suddenly grew extremely tired, and I found it impossible to go any farther. I was still a good distance away from the house, so simply turning back was not an option. I found myself on my knees, crawling and asking for help.

Uncle Robbie observed all of this. He drove up in his bulldozer, laughing his head off. He lowered the scooper part of the bulldozer and screamed as loud as he could over the bulldozer engine, "Roll into it so I can drive you home! Just roll into it!" He really asked me to keep rolling myself on the ground like a big ass log until I landed in his bulldozer scooper arm. My Catherine was there, and she couldn't contain her laughter, either. In the midst of their laughter, I was so angry. Even though I was fussing up a storm and asking for help, they still couldn't stop laughing. Uncle Robbie eventually turned off the engine so he could hear me, but he just ended up laughing again, so much so that he had tears in his eyes. He composed himself after some time, enough so that he could go get his truck to take me home, but he still had residual laughter in his system. He said he knew I wouldn't make it around the lake and that he'd have to come and get me.

He was such a kind man. He told me that if ever I decided to get married, that he would pay for my wedding. "It's on me!" he would say. He had a beautiful yard and said that he would fix it up to accommodate my wedding. He conceded that I would never marry, as in his eyes, I was never serious about anyone. He would often tell me how pretty I was, and he even well-meaningfully offered to buy me a new outfit for every ten pounds I lost. I declined the offer, saying it wasn't enough. He reconsidered and said he would give me his credit card to spend whatever I wanted. I told him that there was another option: that he could just love me as I was and save his money.

I remember I was at church once, sitting next to Uncle Robbie's wife. The pastor told us to stand up and hold hands. I stood up, and Uncle Robbie's wife kept pulling at my arm. She kept pulling, and pulling, and pulling. I wondered what the hell was wrong with her. I told her if she pulled my arm one more time I was going to knock her out. She looked down at me and said, "Oh, I'm sorry. I thought you were still sitting down!" Being all of 4'10", I'm so short that she couldn't fathom the idea that I was already on my feet.

I loved Uncle Robbie so much. He never let anyone bother me, and everyone knew he was my protector. After Uncle Robbie died, I received a phone call from my friend Lola, who I thought was calling to offer her condolences. Instead, I heard, "What are you going to do now? Your backbone is gone. They're really gonna beat your ass everyday now." In the midst of mourning my wonderful Uncle Robbie, my friend brought a little lightness and laughter.

Chapter Thirteen
The Family Bicycle

Getting a new bicycle is one of the joys of childhood. A bicycle can grant children the opportunity to explore their surroundings, to venture out a bit, and to discover the world from a new perspective.

My father, rest his soul, wanted his children to experience all the joys and benefits that come with having a new bike. There were five of us, however, and during those times it was not economically feasible for my father to buy a bike for each of us. So, in all his wisdom and practicality, he bought one bike to be shared by five children. This meant constant fights.

Jimmy claimed sole ownership of the bike and the rest of us, no matter how much we protested, never seemed to receive our fair share of riding time.

When my father first presented the bike to us, we were told in no uncertain terms that the bike was for us, and that we were not permitted to give our friends access to the bike under any circumstances. "Not everybody will take good care of your things the way you do, so don't let anybody else ride this bike." Enter Jimmy's friend Larry, who admired the bike and asked him repeatedly to let him take it for a ride.

We noticed frequently that Larry had greater access to the bike than any of us had. Jimmy just couldn't say "no" to Larry because he was and remains to this day a softhearted soul, and after being asked repeatedly by Larry to let him ride the bike, he relented. Larry rode frequently, leaving little time for the rest of us to get our fair share of riding time. My father silently observed this, but said nothing.

One day, Larry came over and pleaded with Jimmy to let him ride the bike, and again Jimmy handed the bike over. Larry rode the bike downhill and crashed it. The bike's frame was damaged beyond repair, and the front wheel was bent like a taco. Larry and Jimmy pushed the damaged bike uphill and brought it back home.

By allowing Larry to ride our bike, Jimmy had violated the terms and conditions under which my father had given it to us. He warned us that no one would take the proper care and concern for the bike that we would. He further told us that if the bike was damaged by one of our friends, it was unlikely that the other child's parents would be able to make restitution for any damage they caused. Jimmy knew that he was in trouble. My father took the switch to him that night. My father reminded Jimmy that rules were made for a reason. I hated it for Jimmy, but I was glad it wasn't me.

Chapter Fourteen
Minnie's Thrilling Ride

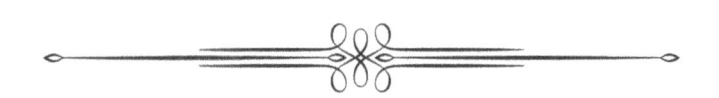

Of my four siblings, Minnie is the oldest. When we were children, whenever our parents went away, they would leave Minnie in charge of the rest of us. She took her role very seriously and would try to assert her authority over us. She would always order us around. She even went so far as calling herself giving Jimmy a whipping with a switch once, which meant she tapped him on his backside. When she tried to order Jason around, however, he would stop her in her tracks. "You ain't my mama!" She knew I wouldn't hesitate to fight her, so she never tried me.

As siblings do, we often found ourselves divided into teams against each other, with Minnie and Jimmy sticking together against Chuck, Jason, and me. No matter what, Jimmy was steadfast in his position on Minnie's team and rarely, if ever, wavered from her side. When our parents arrived back home, each team had a story to tell against the other team.

Another thing about Minnie is that back then, she was a bit of a daredevil. She would often swing on the door casing and yell like Tarzan, even after our father told her to stop before she got hurt. She persisted. One day as she was swinging from the door casing, she fell and hurt her foot. My father's response was, "I told you to stop. Now you done hurt your foot. I'll tell you what, you're still going to hop your ass to the bus stop to go to school tomorrow. A hard head makes a soft ass." Fearing a whipping, Minnie repeatedly insisted that she was all right. There were no emergency rooms at that time, and the doctor's office was closed. My parents wrapped her foot, and she hopped around for days. My mother examined the foot again after a few days and determined that Minnie had actually broken her foot, and she was taken to the doctor.

I want to take a short detour here because thinking about my father telling Minnie she would still have to go to school with an injured foot made me think of something else about him. He always insisted that we be on our best behavior at school. On report card day, we would run home, excited to show off our grades. My father usually seemed more interested in our classroom citizenship behavior than in any of our other grades. He would reach for our report cards and say, "Let me see what you got in 'shut up,' 'cause shutting up is the least you can do in school." My mother would tell him, "No Gib. It's called 'behavior' not 'shut up'!"

"Nawl Gal, I gotta see how these churren doing in 'shut up' over at that school!" We found this very funny.

On some winter mornings, we found ourselves braving the cold temperatures while waiting for the school bus to arrive. My father would walk us to the bus stop, use twigs to ignite a modest fire to keep us warm, and wait with us until we were safely on the warm bus.

And now, back to Minnie. She always liked to do whatever the boys were doing, and one day, Jimmy somehow came to be in possession of a motorbike and was showing it off to the rest of us. It was a nice bike, and it set Minnie's imagination stirring.

She wanted to take it for a ride, but Jimmy told her that the bike didn't have any brakes—that she would have to wait until the bike was fixed because it was too dangerous to ride in its present state. Minnie wouldn't let up. She continued asking him to let her ride the bike and eventually, Jimmy relented, even though it was against his better judgment.

The bike was a bit small for Minnie, but she didn't care about that, nor did she care about the fact that it didn't have brakes. The motorbike had a handle that was used to regulate the speed. The further the handle was pulled out from its original position, the faster the motorbike would go.

Minnie knew the bike had no brakes, but still, she hopped on and pulled the speed handle out as far as it would go. A burst of uncontrollable laughter sprang out from Chuck, Jason, and me, because suddenly, Minnie was screaming frantically at the top of her lungs as she found herself jetting down the dirt road through the woods at maximum speed. Her legs were outstretched from the sides of the too-small-for-her bike, but she maneuvered the bike masterfully and it was a wonder to see her dodge tree after tree while bushes, branches, and twigs lashed out at her extended legs.

At top speed, as Minnie meandered her way screaming through the woods, Jimmy, who could run with the speed of a cheetah racing through the Savannah, chased after her, screaming "Jump off, jump off, Minnie, jump off!" It was to no avail because between the sound coming from the bike's motor and the howling laughter from the rest of us, Minnie couldn't hear him.

Jimmy eventually caught up to the bike and pulled Minnie off to safety. He was so angry with her for taking off so fast, and for not taking "No" for an answer when she first asked him to ride. He yelled at her, saying, "I told you the bike didn't have brakes. I told you! You could've killed yourself." Seeing how afraid and shaken she was, Jason softened and hugged her. "You'll be all right." He was relieved, too.

Chapter Fifteen
Easter Sunday and the Christmas Play

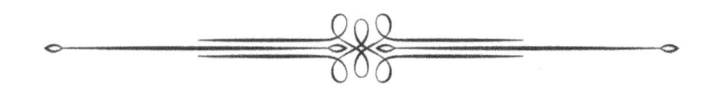

During my early childhood, Easter Sunday was a special occasion. We always dressed up for church. I remember one particular Easter Sunday when I had to wear a dress that I absolutely hated. This dress was made of taffeta-like material, the kind that was used to give the old "Can Can" dresses structure and volume, and it left me scratching every minute, it seemed, that I had it on. Not only that, the damned dress was clearly and obviously much too small for me, adding to my discomfort. They also made me wear a damned pair of slippery, patent leather shoes. There's no way they could've thought I looked cute in that dress and shoes.

On top of all that, I had to wear the same clothes to school the following Monday. Thank goodness there are no pictures, but if there were, I know I would probably laugh at how ridiculous they made me look that Sunday.

Another thing about Easter Sunday is that we would have to frequently do recitations. For this particular Easter, we were assigned poems to be performed in front of everyone, poems my mother insisted that we recite perfectly.

Even after all these years, I still remember the poem that was designated for me. It read: "Roses on my shoulders, slippers on my feet, I am my daddy's baby child, and don't you think I'm sweet?" Yes, they made me say that.

Two of my brothers had to recite as well, with one of them having to stand up and say: "I may not be a curly-headed boy and my dad is not a preacher, but I like to go to Sunday school to listen at the teacher." The second brother had to actually say these words: "What you looking at me so hard for? I didn't come to stay. I just come to say, today is Easter day."

You can just imagine the laughter and applause we received. My mother was so proud. It was her children up there entertaining the congregation on that Easter Sunday. She hugged and kissed us, smiling from ear to ear. She knew she nearly had to beat us to death to learn those poems.

Come Monday morning, we had to wear those same clothes to school; me, in those slippery patent leather shoes and that uncomfortable, too-small-for-me scratchy dress! I will always cherish my childhood Easter Sundays. Let's not even talk about the eggs, though!

For many children, Christmas is a wonderful, cherished time of year. The sentiment extends beyond families and into school systems as well, where the festive season brings about a unique sense of joy, particularly among young children. As a child, I was extremely happy to take part in the annual school Christmas play. One year, on that eventful night, it was exciting to know that my family would be in the audience watching me perform. I felt proud to be on that stage. The school that I attended five days a week was suddenly transformed into a magical wonderland, and I was eager to give a great performance. As the curtain opened, my heart raced with excitement. I knew this would be something I would remember forever.

Well, it was memorable that's for sure, but not in the way I expected it to be. My brother Jason sitting on my mother's lap out in the audience was caught up in the excitement too. He spotted me among my classmates on the stage and shouted, "There go Yang Yang!" He screamed again repeatedly, and by this time, the audience had erupted with laughter. I realized that the only way I was going to get my brother to shut up was to wave at him from the stage.

My aunt who also came to the school that night to see the program was noticeably intoxicated. When Jason shouted, "Yang Yang," she burst into uncontrollable laughter and fell off her chair, kneeling in front of it as though she were praying, but she was laughing. It caused quite a commotion in the auditorium, and after what felt like an eternity, the chaos settled and the show resumed as planned. However, as the curtain closed at the end of the performance, there was a minor disturbance backstage. Young Jason yelled at the top of his lungs, "Yang Yang done fell!" I so wished he had stayed home. All those people there…why in his mind did it have to be me who fell? His outburst started a whole other wave of laughter among the audience. It was incredibly embarrassing for me, and I dreaded going to school the next day, knowing that my classmates would tease me about it relentlessly. That damn Jason!

Chapter Sixteen
Murphy the Trickster

With a boisterous group of my four siblings and the added presence of my mischievous cousins, our hang-outs at home were a time of fun and laughter. We thrived on playful banter, teasing one another, but all in good fun. Pranks were common among us, and it did you no good to have thin skin. Occasionally, we found ourselves at the receiving end of a joke or prank. Laughter was the glue that bound us together. Whenever we were or are together, laughter was and is guaranteed.

Among my cousins, there was one individual who possessed an extraordinary talent for making us laugh. That was Murphy, immortalized in the photograph on page _____. May he rest in peace. With an innate gift for humor, Murphy could effortlessly make me laugh. During our younger years, he had difficulty pronouncing my name, Mary Ann. Instead, he affectionately referred to me as "Yang Yang." I wasn't particularly fond of this nickname, but out of empathy, I accepted it, understanding his struggle to articulate my name correctly. I reluctantly embraced the nickname, believing it to be due to a genuine speech impediment or some form of linguistic challenge he was dealing with. In my efforts to accommodate him, I responded to the name whenever he called me.

However, one fateful day, the truth was unveiled before my eyes. I stumbled upon another young girl in our town who bore the name

Mary Ann—an identical appellation to my own. In a strange turn of events, Murphy's previously elusive tongue suddenly acquired the ability to flawlessly pronounce "Mary Ann." A miraculous transformation had occurred and granted him mastery over the pronunciation of my name. A miracle? Far from it! Murphy had been pulling the wool over my eyes the whole time. A surge of anger washed over me. I felt deceived and a bit gullible for falling for his lie. Initially, I was furious with him. How dare he maintain such an elaborate prank? My anger subsided. What could I do about it anyway? The nickname was already stuck on me.

As I mentioned previously, having a thin skin was simply not an option in my family. It was and remains to this day a world where the ability to deliver witty remarks and clever comebacks was and is highly valued. Equally important is the capacity to handle such playful exchanges in stride.

At any given moment, you run the risk of being subjected to a diss, a sly put-down, or finding yourself the subject of a prank. In this environment, the art of teasing was an essential part of our family bond. Taunting each other and quick-witted playful insults were the norm. It was a method by which we showed affection toward one another.

Each of us had to develop quick thinking and a sharp sense of humor and have the ability to respond creatively to whatever came our way. Being able to hold one's own when it came to jokes and pranks in my family was and remains an essential skill. Through this kind of play over the years, we have deepened our bond and our sense of unity.

Chapter Seventeen
Pranksters Catherine and Dallis

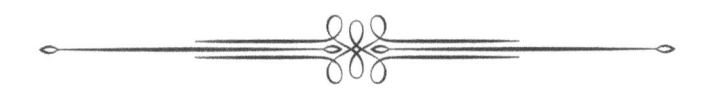

My daughter Catherine was the bright star in my father's universe. He absolutely adored and cherished her. He called her his "Block house!" He would go to great lengths to indulge her whims, even allowing her to play hairstylist and have full control over his hair from time to time.

Catherine, armed with a jar of hair grease, would transform her grandfather's head into a shining, sleek ball. As she worked, she would position his head in oddly contorted angles, making his neck bend in very unnatural and uncomfortable ways. Yet not a single complaint escaped my father's lips. He endured the discomfort of Catherine's salon with calmness and complacency, all for the sake of his beloved granddaughter's amusement.

I would occasionally interject, "No, Catherine! You're hurting your grandpa!" But my father, in his infinite wisdom, would simply wave off my well-intentioned warnings. "Let her be!" he would insist. He had made a decision to endure any ordeal in this hairstyle process for the sake of his special bond with his granddaughter. And so the spectacle continued. Catherine would navigate her comb through his thick hair, each stroke as if she were taming a wild animal atop her grandpa's head.

The wild tugs and erratic strokes notwithstanding, Grandpa continued to smile and to humor Catherine, who was totally engrossed in her work. My father would endure it all for his "Block house." I loved seeing their special bond. While I wanted to intervene more and to rescue my father from further turmoil, I couldn't deny the harmony that existed between them.

Young Catherine, bless her mischievous soul, also had a knack for pulling pranks, and who better to target than her doting and unsuspecting grandfather?

One of her all-time favorite pranks was playing "The Wrong Number Game" with her dear old grandpa, only he never seemed to catch on. Whenever he innocently asked for someone's number when he wanted to make a phone call, she would seize the opportunity to unleash her mischievous genius on the situation. In answer to his question, she would rattle off with confidence digits that could have easily belonged to just about anyone except for who her grandfather wanted to reach.

My unsuspecting father, bursting with enthusiasm, would look forward to talking to his friend. Little did he know, his cherished conversation with his buddy Sam was not going to happen. Instead it would be interrupted by the bewildered voice of a complete stranger. "Hello?" they would say, only to be met with my father's classic line in this situation: "Oh, I'm sorry!"

It became a recurring comedy routine in our household, and Catherine reveled in the symphony of apologies from my father to those on the other end of the line. He never caught on to the fact that his darling granddaughter was the mastermind behind this deliberate tomfoolery. He would be exasperated, but he kept seeking her assistance in a quest for the "right" numbers. We couldn't help but wonder, "Why does he keep subjecting himself to this craziness?"

One day he jokingly threatened Catherine, "If you give me the wrong number again, I'm going to beat your little fat ass!" We laughed at this absurdity. Catherine, fearless as ever, simply shrugged and replied, "How was I supposed to memorize all those numbers, Grandpa? I don't even remember where I left my socks!"

And so the saga continued. Grandpa persistently sought out phone numbers, and Catherine delighted in providing him with a cocktail of confusion. No spanking or "beating of little fat asses" ever ensued, of course. It was all in good fun, a dance of love and laughter between a grandfather and his beloved granddaughter. And while the telephone lines of unsuspecting people bore the brunt of this absurd routine between grandfather and granddaughter, it provided our house with so much laughter.

When Catherine was a little older, my goddaughter Dallis, along with her two young children, came to live with us for a short time. Dallis reminded me of myself when I was a younger woman raising two children on my own, and she was doing a great job. She is a lovely, intelligent woman and by heaven, she sings like an angel. Her voice is among the most beautiful I have ever heard in my life. She sang "Happy Birthday" to me one year. Never in my life had I heard it sung so stunningly beautifully as Dallis had sang it for me. It moved me to tears and I will never forget her rendition.

Back then, Dallis was also a bit of a jokester. On the weekends, she teamed up frequently with my daughter Catherine and they got up to all kinds of trickery and pranks, being thoroughly amused by people's reactions.

One year, our local news station promoted an exciting contest offering participants the chance to win a coveted "Date With Dale." There was always much talk about this elusive prize and most everywhere you went, there was talk of who the latest winner was and who might win in the future.

Enter pranksters Dallis and Catherine. They masterminded a plan and set out to execute it with precision. Once their gameplan was hatched, they decided Dallis would take center stage for this one. She cunningly disguised her voice and called my Aunt Laura, posing as a representative of the local news station delivering exciting news: Aunt Laura had won the highly sought after "Date With Dale" contest.

As you can imagine, Aunt Laura was overjoyed. She had never won anything in her life and this triumph became extra special to her. There was one caveat to the contest. In order to claim the prize, Aunt Laura first had to sing, in its entirety, the song "Children Go Where I Send Thee." Fortunately, Aunt Laura knew the song (as the pranksters well knew), so as far as she was concerned, her "Date With Dale" was in the bag. Aunt Laura took a deep breath and began singing the lyrics from beginning to end.

The song is a traditional African American spiritual Christmas song that tells the story of the birth of Jesus Christ through a culmination of one by one, all the way through to ten by ten—quite a long song. Aunt Laura sang the entire song, each and every line, making it really difficult for Dallis and Catherine to contain their laughter as they held the mouthpiece of the phone tightly. They huddled together with the phone between them, listening and laughing, knowing that they had succeeded in the ultimate prank.

Chapter Eighteen
The Tithes Story

My father had a wonderful sense of humor, and he could always elicit laughter from all those around him. He was a great hunter who drew in men from other counties, not only so they could learn about hunting from him, but also largely because they wanted to experience the fun and humor my father always brought with him. He was the kind of person people always wanted to be around, and as a result, our house was very often full of laughter from his friends. I hope that I have shared with you enough bits and pieces as to create a nice glimpse into just what a jovial, lighthearted, funny man my father was.

I would be remiss if I didn't share with you the time that my dear father, who only went to church on special occasions, always dressed to the nines mind you, threatened to go to church to beat the hell out of the preacher.

You see, back in those days, the church would send an emissary to your house once a month to collect your offering or tithes, usually in the amount of two dollars. Well, during those times, two dollars was nothing to sneeze at. The church representative came around regularly enough to collect my father's two dollars, however, my father's name ended up on the infamous list of those who had not paid—a list which was prominently displayed in the church hall for everyone to see.

I'm not a hundred percent sure, but perhaps the church thought that this list of shame was the most effective way they could think of to get people to unlock their wallets. It was a subtle way of coercing people to pay, under threat that their name would be publicly displayed as some kind of delinquent. The church people also knew that the list gave people something to gossip about. It was essentially a list of shame, and it didn't sit well with my father.

Somehow my father got word that his name had been placed on the delinquent payment list. He was furious when he heard this. He cussed and ranted and raved all through the house. "Sending somebody 'round here to get my damn money, two dollars, and she done spent my damn money. That ain't gon' work! She bring her ass around here next month we gon' have a talk."

He was dead serious, but we found it funny, and we couldn't stop laughing. He said, "Shit like that make me hot! You wait till she brings her ass back round here next month asking for two dollars. We sho gon' have a talk! Got my name on a list on a damn wall out there for all these folks to see. I may not go to church, but the Master knows I pay my goddam two dollars!"

He was so angry, and we just found it all so funny, we kept laughing. "I'm going to church next fourth Sunday, and if I see my name on that list, I might just beat the preacher's ass for spending my money and putting my name up there for folks to see!" In those days, people were proud to pay their offering to the church. They believed that they were somehow giving to God. It was a sacrifice they made proudly, but the wall of shame was a way to keep people in check, so to speak.

When fourth Sunday finally came, my father was ready—looking good (as he always did whenever he went anywhere), smelling good, but still ready to beat the preacher's ass if necessary. I couldn't wait to see the showdown. "Daddy gon' beat up the preacher!" That was the only reason I wanted to go. I was excited. I didn't want to miss the showdown. I got dressed hurriedly so I wouldn't miss a single thing. When we arrived, my father, who couldn't read, was very serious. He asked me to read the list and tell him if his name was there. "I can't Daddy, I'm too short! I can't see it."

As it turned out, someone had warned the people in the church that my father had been told about his name being on the list. They were also told that he, who rarely came to church, would be there on the fourth Sunday to "say his piece." They heeded the warning, and my father's name was nowhere to be seen on the list.

Over the years, people who knew my father have told me that I inherited his sense of humor. I don't doubt this, as I myself love to laugh, and I love it when people around me are also able to laugh. There's enough and strife in this world to keep us down and dejected for centuries to come. We all know this. However, if this is the only life that we know of, and if we can find laughter within ourselves from time to time and share that laughter with others, I think it makes life all the more enjoyable, and I'm all for that.

One of my father's favorite songs was "Oh Mary Don't You Weep." He sang it all the time. Another one of his favorites was "Chain of Fools" by Aretha Franklin. However, my daddy never sang the lyrics right, and when my mother was mad at him, he'd sing, "Change, change, change, change, change, change, can't change a fool." If it's true that a sense of humor can be passed down from generation to generation, then I think the apple didn't fall far from the tree in my case, either.

I have written before about my daughter Catherine and her propensity for pranks and laughter, but growing up, she was also very caring and very affectionate toward her cousins. She took the utmost care when she would bathe her little cousins, but she was a bit heavy-handed when it came to the hair grease and lotion. She would grease the child so much that you could barely pick them up because they were slippery. From head to toe they would be covered in grease. One day, she offered her cousin the opportunity to make him look cool for school. He liked that idea and let her go to work on his hair. Her idea to make him look cool was to grease his hair down until it was super slick. He ended up with a head full of pure grease, and he had to hurry and wash it out before his school bus came. She did the same thing to her cheerleader niece, Rita. Grease and sun don't mix well. Catherine put so much grease in Rita's hair before a football game that when Rita was out there cheering on the sideline, the sun cooked the grease in her head until it was melting down the sides of her face and neck. Her poor scalp! Loving and well-meaning Aunt Catherine had struck again.

Chapter Nineteen
For the Love of Baseball

As a sharecropper as well as in his work that would come later, my father had a strong work ethic. From the first rise of the early morning sun to the gentle descent into evening, he immersed himself in the earth, planting and tending to the crops that nourished us. Through the sweat on his brow and the calluses on his hands, he was the spirit of determination that characterized the sharecropping way of life to support his family.

The lifestyle of a sharecropper was physically demanding. Still, my father toiled under the sun-drenched skies and poured his heart into cultivating the fertile fields that sustained our family.

With every seed he sowed and every crop he tended, I like to think that his major focus was always the well-being of our family and a hope for a better future for all of us.

Yes, my father worked hard to coax abundance from the earth, important skills he also taught to us.

Through sweltering summers and bone-chilling winters, he worked through it all. He persisted and prevailed in the face of all of nature's whims.

Later in life, he held a position at the Department of Transportation, and then sometime later he was fortunate enough to get a good position with Georgia Craft, from which he retired.

After he retired he never wanted to sit down, so he got a job at the local recycling plant. My father couldn't read, but he sure could count, especially money. I was a teacher, but he made more money than I did, and he loved to show off. If on occasion I was too late to catch the bank before it closed on payday, my father would proudly cash my paychecks for me. He would loan other people money from time to time, but he insisted that they pay him back with interest.

As you can tell, I loved and revered my father. There are so many things that I remember about him that I could fill this book with stories just about him.

My father loved baseball and he was a phenomenal player.

He passed his love for the sport down to his sons and grandsons, most notably in the local Hall of Fame record held by my son—his grandson, from the heyday of Andrew's high school years.

Andrew made such a name for himself that his jersey is now retired. His record-breaking skills on the baseball field earned him trophy after trophy and award after award. His record remains unmatched, and to this day, I still have the numerous trophies and awards he earned in school. How could he be otherwise, given that he was well trained in baseball by his uncles and his grandfather even before he started school? The great talent that he demonstrated on the baseball field was a genetic gift passed down to him from the paternal side of my family, but he also excelled in football.

It is far from a stretch to say that my father could have been drafted into the major leagues. He played frequently with "Blue Moon Odom," a wonderful player from Macon, Georgia, who actually did go on to play Major League Baseball with the Kansas City Athletics in 1964. It was always said that my father, too, could have been drafted as he was every bit the professional pitcher that Odom was, with Odom very likely using techniques he closely observed from my father as they played on the same baseball field, even though my father was several years Odom's senior. My paternal grandparents, with good reason, were fearful, however. You see, my father couldn't read, and the racial climate being what it was at the time, his parents were afraid to allow him to travel with any sports team. They were afraid that he might be killed on the road and that if he left home, they would never see him alive again.

Still, his talent on the pitcher's mound was legendary. He masterfully struck people out and it was always something to behold. I know that my father would have done the professional leagues proud. His skilled technique confused the batters to the point where they never knew what to expect. He would take a stance as though he was going to throw the ball hard and fast, but it turned out his pitch was as soft as if he was pitching to a baby, and the batter was thrown completely off his game.

He taught my brother Jimmy how to pitch, showing off his auto didactic trade secrets of how to throw a knuckle ball and a curve ball effectively to always keep batters guessing and unstable.

The baseball field where my father played was a pecan field that White people had given him permission to use.

People would come from other towns to play. As I mentioned, my father was the pitcher, and the catcher was a local guy named "Old Jack" who loved to drink on Saturday nights. The games were mostly held on Sunday. Old Jack would yell to the pitcher, "Throw it hard now, throw it hard!" It seemed the drunker Old Jack was, the better he could catch. He played better drunk than most people played sober. Jack's daughter played on our girls' team, and even she would laugh about her father being drunk out there on the catcher's mound. For us, sports and laughter went hand in hand.

Chapter Twenty
Saying Goodbye to Daddy

Saying a final goodbye to my father was one of the hardest things I've ever had to do in my life. He was a good man and I loved him very much. He was respected in our community, and at his funeral there were just as many White people there as there were Black people.

The White man who owned the local garage gave remarks at the service, speaking of my father with utmost respect and the highest esteem. It is important to me that I take the time to acknowledge him because he and his family never hid behind the convictions about never showing kindness to Black people. He even called my mother "Grandma." That my mother accepted his calling her "Grandma" spoke to her heart of forgiveness. I am grateful to them for showing kindness and respect to both of my parents, and for recognizing and honoring them with the esteem they deserved.

For all that my parents endured in the early twentieth century as Black people in the Southern United States, forgiveness was always in their hearts. You must remember that during the historical periods of legal racial discrimination, segregation, and Jim Crow laws up to the 1950s and beyond, there were social and cultural norms that imposed limitations on the interactions between White people and Black people. These norms were rooted in racial prejudice and their purpose was to maintain the oppressive power dynamics that existed at the time. Under these conditions, White people were often expected to uphold and reinforce the prevailing racial hierarchy, which placed White individuals at the top and marginalized Black people.

This meant that White people had to be cautious about publicly showing any form of kindness, care, or empathy toward Black people. The fear was that such acts might be perceived as challenging the racial status quo and could result in backlash, ostracism, or even physical harm from other White individuals who were committed to maintaining those racial norms of the time. Demonstrating care or concern for the comfort of Black people was risky for Whites at that time.

The consequences of being seen as too kind or sympathetic toward Black people varied depending on the specific time and place, but they could range from social isolation and ridicule to loss of employment, harassment, or violence. These pressures created a climate of fear and enforced silence among White individuals who may have genuinely felt empathy toward Black people or those who wanted to challenge racial injustice.

I felt that this was an important point to make because my parents, my family, and I lived it and it continues today in its own subtle, and sometimes not so subtle, form. I have seen it up close and deeply personally, and I have felt deeply the hurt and pain it causes. I feel it necessary to acknowledge and understand this history. May we all commit to dismantling "otherness," and to promoting love, kindness, and understanding.

Chapter Twenty-One
Larry the Catcher

The merciless sun made it extremely hot and humid, with no air or breeze to be felt anywhere out on the baseball field one afternoon. We loved our sports then as we do now, and we weathered the unrelenting Georgia sun for the sake of baseball whenever we had to. On one especially hot summer day, we were out at the baseball field for a game.

Larry, an exceptional catcher who could've easily turned pro if he had the opportunity, was crouched behind home plate. He abruptly stood up and started cussing, pacing wildly, and flailing his arms about as we looked on, wondering what in the world was wrong with him. He began throwing off his clothes, screaming, "The bear got me! The bear got me!" We had no idea what was really happening, so we just thought he might be drunk. My father ran to him and guided him to try and find shade under a nearby tree. Everybody was fanning Larry and as my father explained to us that the sun had become too much for Larry and that he was feeling the harmful effects of overexposure, someone suggested throwing water on him.

My father said "No" to this, telling us that the best course of action was for him to sip cool water and to stay under the tree so that his temperature would gradually and steadily return to normal. After some time, Larry was back on his feet, but he had to take it easy for a bit. The school year started, and Larry's son was in my class. He was a handful to say the least. He wouldn't stay seated, and he disrupted the class with frequent outbursts. I was successful in getting him to calm down because he knew that I knew his father. It was the time of year when teachers had to call the student's parents for the annual teacher-parent conference.

I have said much here about my beloved daughter Catherine and her propensity for pranks during her younger years. I suppose at this point I have to acknowledge the fact that the apple doesn't fall far from the tree because I, myself, have been known to pull the occasional prank.

One such prank was on Larry. I called his house, using a disguised voice. "Mr. Larry?" I said. "Yes ma'am?" he answered.

"I'm your son's teacher, Ms. Jefferson."

"How do you do, ma'am?"

"Well, I'm calling to tell you that your son is the baddest child in this whole damned school. He acts out because he lacks discipline at home, and this is a real problem."

"Nawl, nawl now! You got me fucked up! You call *my* house with that shit?" was his reply.

"Well, if you feel that way sir, you need to come to the school tomorrow," I said.

"I will. I won't even go to work tomorrow. I'll be there first thing in the morning!" he said. At that point, I could no longer contain my laughter about our heated exchange. I burst out laughing so much until I felt weak. I had to pass the phone to Jimmy. At that point, Larry caught my real voice. "This you, Yang? I'll be damned! You got me!" We laughed so much. He was like a brother to me, and I miss him dearly. He did come to the school the next day. We laughed again but he was sure to tell his son, "Quit acting like a damned fool!"

Chapter Twenty-Two
Donnie and Murphy: Baseball Domination

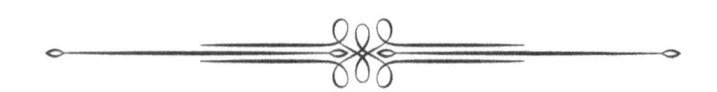

Donnie and Murphy were brothers. They were not twins, but they were both born the same year, one in January, the other in December. In our southern rural world of baseball, Donnie and Murphy stood out. One played pitcher while the other played catcher. Their subtle communication signals on the field were legendary. They were both really remarkable players, with each possessing their own self-styled brand of athleticism. It was Donnie, however, who truly mesmerized everyone with his keen ability to use both hands with equal dexterity. He used his ambidexterity to his advantage whenever he was up to bat and to throw.

We would all be on the edge of our seats, eagerly awaiting Donnie's turn at bat. When he stepped up to the plate, all eyes were on him. We knew he would do something remarkable. He would effortlessly hit the ball out of the park, over fences and over trees. Even after all the years that have passed, Donnie's prowess with the bat is still discussed from time to time, with people saying things like, "He hit that ball so hard it's *still* in the air." Both brothers, Donnie and Murphy, were such gifted baseball players. The coaches counted on their talents so much, and as I recall, even when they were absent, the coaches would find them to get them to go to practice. They just couldn't do without Donnie and Murphy's skills out on the baseball field.

Donnie was like another son to my father. He adored my father and my father had mutually fond feelings for him. Donnie would even imitate Daddy's impeccable fashion sense. My father always liked to dress well wherever he went, and his gold pinky ring was always a must-have accessory. In many of the pictures I have of him, you will find him wearing a suit. He relished getting dressed for special occasions, with white being his favorite color. I miss them all every day. Rest in peace Daddy, Murphy, and Donnie. I love you.

We enjoyed watching the boys play baseball, but we girls also had our athletic talents. Some of us were very good too—with the exception of one girl who tried out for our awesome girls' team. She showed up in her bifocal glasses with yet another lens glued to them. She also had her baseball glove, and from our observation, we really thought that she was going to make a great effort. She seemed athletic and really ready to do the job until the first fly ball came her way. The ball was in the air, headed straight for her glove. We all watched and waited for what we knew would be an easy out.

All she had to do was step back and let the ball fall into her gloved hand. As it turned out, the ball didn't land in her glove. It landed perfectly on top of her head. My sister Minnie fell out rolling on the field, laughing at what we had just seen. When the ball hit, the girl exclaimed at the top of her voice "That's *it!*" She threw down her glove and was storming off the baseball field when we all ran to her to see about her injury; was she hurt? Did she need a doctor? All except Minnie. Minnie was still on the ground laughing. The incident and the imagery of how it all happened kept her in stitches for so long, and she still brings it up from time to time even after all these years.

Chapter Twenty-Three
Rita, My Angel

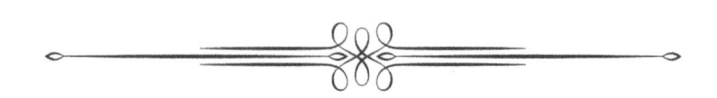

My lovely granddaughter Rita! What an angel, a blessing she is to me. As a little girl, she always made the most precious cards for me, and she wrote me the sweetest notes. She really loved the song "We Will, We Will Rock You," by the group Queen. Her aunt Catherine and I had to sing it with her all the time. Rita was entered in a pageant to be Miss Crawford County when she was a child. She wore the most beautiful white dress, and she looked as lovely as ever.

The funny thing is, it really didn't matter to her whether she won the pageant or not, so she didn't take it seriously at all. Her father Andrew told her she was a winner whether she won or not. I, on the other hand, was your typical stage grandmother. I wanted the win. I wanted nothing more than for her to win, and I certainly didn't want her to get up there and embarrass me. Over and over again, I insisted that she practice her lines and give it her all, which she just wasn't too keen to do. I would rant and rave about her practicing her lines, while she and her aunt Catherine would just go in another room and laugh at how ridiculous I was being.

The pageant stage at school was decorated beautifully with nice furniture, which included a very dainty lady's vanity to give the effect of Rita being at home. Asked why she thought she should win, Rita adorably replied, "Because I'm sugar and spice and everything nice."

Once during a practice at the school, a man who lived in the community hopped up on stage out of the blue. He insisted on offering his unsolicited assistance to help Rita with the contest. I believe it is possible that he may have heard some negative talk from some of the adults associated with the pageant about Rita's chances of winning. You could tell that he was feeling pretty good from the night before because you could smell the "Kool-Aid" on his breath.

It was both funny and shocking as he began coaching Rita and directing her movements, telling her in his slurred speech to turn around this way and then that way in true pageant form, and to "do the Harlem Shake right there." You could tell that Rita, all of six or seven years old, was wondering who the hell this man was. However, she followed his directions as we looked on, trying to hold back laughter.

Then, after she had posed this way and that according to his unsolicited coaching instructions, right then and there he declared her the winner. "She won. The contest is over. That girl is pretty and sweet. No need to come back here next week. Take away all that furniture and clear the stage because this girl already won." He told Rita, who couldn't possibly care less about the pageant, "If you don't win, I wanna know why. They're gonna have to answer to me." Then, without another word, the kindly man was gone.

We knew this guy's reputation, and it is not a stretch to suggest that he wanted to quickly get through the practice so that he could get back to his regular activities. It was just one of those really weird things, and we found it so funny.

As with any pageant, later there was a town parade wherein a red Ford Mustang convertible was made available for Rita, and she rode through town sitting like a little princess high up on the back seat. I knew the owner of the Mustang, and I remain grateful that he so graciously drove my little princess ever so slowly around the town so that everyone could see that she was Little Miss Crawford County. She sat there, smiling and waving, and I was so proud.

Chapter Twenty-Four
Chuck's Prized Possession

My brother Chuck was the envy of our town with his beautiful and impressive car. Just how he acquired the vehicle remains a mystery to me. Whether he saved his hard-earned money or if it was bestowed upon him as a generous gift from our father, one thing was certain: over the years it would transform into a timeless classic.

This magnificent vehicle, a sleek two-door SS Chevy Malibu with an automatic transmission, boasted a beautiful shade of blue. Chuck's dedication to maintaining its prime condition was evident in the car's flawless exterior.

One day, he felt that it was time to breathe new life into his prized possession though, and he made the decision to give it a fresh coat of paint.

It wasn't long before acquaintances, friends, and even strangers found themselves glancing at the remarkable sight of this incredible car. Chuck was proud of his car and relished every moment as owner of this automotive masterpiece.

People were captivated by the car's charm and elegance. Passersby stopped and admired the paint job and the smooth lines of the Chevy Malibu. The car had become a symbol of Chuck's unique taste, and he was meticulous about the care and upkeep of the vehicle. He was devoted to his car and would never eat in it while he was behind the wheel.

Enter Catherine. About five years old, cute as can be, sweet and adorable, but also a bit mischievous. One day, enjoying the outdoors with a playmate, Catherine found herself unable to resist the beauty of Chuck's clean blue car. Perhaps in her young mind, she thought the car lacked only one thing to complete its beauty: her name, which she had only recently learned to write properly.

Being the creative child she was, she gathered her friend and found a nail with which she proceeded to carve her name, in big, bold letters, deep into the car's finish. Her creativity didn't stop there. In a display of fellowship, she passed the nail to her little friend, who also carved her name onto Chuck's prized possession, in letters equally as bold and large. Their mischievous collaboration project was now finished, and they were completely oblivious to the damage they had caused. Shocked and totally devastated by the horrific damage those two little girls wrought upon his blue SS Chevy Malibu with the new paint job, Chuck was distraught. He had no alternative. Exasperated and utterly defeated, he asked, "Do I have permission to whoop Catherine's little ass?" Well, Catherine's little ass was whooped that day. I'm happy to say that the damage was reparable, and Chuck was able to restore his prized possession back to its former glory.

Chapter Twenty-Five
The Family Huntsmen

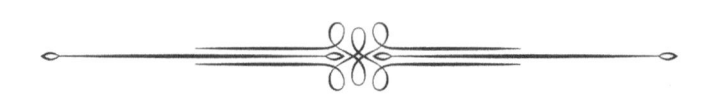

My father and my brothers shared a deep passion for hunting, a cherished tradition that connected them to the land and provided sustenance for our family. Living in the countryside, they were fortunate enough to have a hunting ground right at their doorstep, accessible by simply opening the back door. The dense woods surrounding our home were brimming with opportunities to pursue game and to fill our plates with the fruits of their labor.

While they engaged in hunting all throughout the year, Thanksgiving was a special time for them, and they dedicated the day solely to this exhilarating pursuit. Rising before dawn, my father and brothers would eagerly set out into the woods, accompanied by their hunting dogs. Their main pursuit for the day was rabbit. They geared up with their trusty firearms and ventured into the briars and thickets where these elusive creatures would hide.

The dogs played an important part in their hunting efforts. My father and my brothers counted on the dogs' well-honed instincts and training to sniff out the rabbits hidden in the undergrowth. Their keen noses led the way, guiding my father and brothers to the perfect spots for an ambush. My father, being an expert hunter himself, had passed down his knowledge to my brothers. They were quite experienced hunters with years of practice behind them, and the bond they forged with the hunting dogs was remarkable.

The rabbits they pursued were not mere trophies; they served as a vital source of food for our household. Understanding the importance of preserving the meat, my father meticulously taught my brothers the precise locations to aim for when taking a shot at the animal. The Thanksgiving hunting tradition often resulted in an abundance of rabbits. Such was their success that they would periodically return to the house with their spoils, only to venture out once more to seek additional game. As the designated rabbit cleaner, it was my responsibility to prepare the catch to be cooked by my mother. Over time, I honed my skills and became increasingly efficient in cleaning rabbits.

Word of my father's prowess as a hunter spread far and wide. Men from as far as Atlanta sought the opportunity to join him on hunting expeditions. Rarely refusing their requests, my father would conduct a brief crash course on gun safety to ensure everyone's well-being. The woods could be treacherous, and my father prioritized the safety of his fellow hunters. He imparted the fundamentals of hunting and emphasized the importance of staying clear of another hunter's line of fire. He wanted to keep everyone safe and to ensure a good hunting experience.

One particular incident stands out among the countless hunting adventures my father and my brothers shared with the rest of our family over the years. After a grueling day of pursuit, my father's fatigue had caught up with him. He was tired. His legs gave way, and he found himself unable to continue walking. With miles separating them from the comfort of home, he insisted that my brothers lift him up and carry him back. They balked at the idea, complaining and refusing to even consider the idea. Realizing their reluctance, my father injected a humorous twist into the situation. My brothers knew first-hand what a great shot my father was. From his seated position on the ground, my father playfully threatened them. "I still have my shotgun and I can hit all three of you with a single bullet!" Unsure whether my father was joking, my brothers chose not to take any chances. They lifted him up and carried him back safely to the house, although they were none too happy about doing it.

Upon their return, our family would gather around the table. We would eagerly await the tales of adventure from the day's hunting escapades. Those stories became the centerpiece of our evenings, akin to a riveting television show or even an adventurous movie that would bring the challenges and the tales of the hunt to life right before our eyes. We knew that their return meant we would be treated to a colorful assortment of entertaining anecdotes from the woods.

Among the many riveting tales that breathed life into our family gatherings, another one stood out—the humorous account of Felix, the father of one of my children, who once joined the hunting expedition with my father and my brothers. Felix had no hunting experience whatsoever, but he had a curiosity and a burning desire to partake in the adventure. Following a thorough instructional session on gun safety and all the necessary precautions, my father, accompanied by my brothers, led Felix into the depths of the woods for a day of hunting.

As evening fell and they returned home, the atmosphere around the dinner table crackled with anticipation, knowing that a comical narrative was about to unfold. All eyes turned to Felix, the protagonist of this tale. My father and my brothers chuckled and insisted that Felix tell the tale. They burst out in infectious laughter even before Felix began, which caused everyone else around the table to laugh as well. The laughter swelled before we even knew what happened out in the woods.

The story goes that Felix, armed and equipped with his newfound bravado, stood confident and ready for the hunt. Out of nowhere, a rabbit hopped onto the scene. Not just any rabbit, mind you, but an extremely bold one. This bold rabbit sauntered up to Felix and stood with its hind legs planted firmly on the ground. It was as if the rabbit was daring Felix to shoot him, as it stared him down with bold confidence. It became a showdown between man and bunny. All eyes around the table widened with anticipation as Felix reenacted the encounter. The tension was palpable as Felix recounted the internal struggle he faced in that fleeting moment. His compassionate nature shone through as he was moved by the innocence and charm of the woodland creature. As the rabbit hopped away, evading its potential fate, Felix's heart overruled his desire to be a hunter. He couldn't bring himself to pull the trigger. The bunny had won.

The laughter around the table was so loud it could've raised the roof. My father never let up on Felix. "You came back home with the same amount of shells you left home with!" Just as everyone calmed down, they would be struck again by the imagery of the bunny squaring up in front of Felix, and the laughter flared up all over again. My father and my brothers bombarded Felix with good-natured jibes. "Felix, why didn't you just shoot the damn rabbit?" They could barely string their words together between fits of laughter.

Felix laughed too and attempted to explain himself, with his words tumbling out amid snorts and giggles. "He looked at me with those eyes," he managed to squeeze out between chuckles, "and I just couldn't bear to shoot him." The table erupted in a fresh wave of laughter with the image of Felix caught in the gaze of a bold, fearless, sweet bunny.

The story is recounted frequently, with even greater gusto as it passes from one person to the next. Each retelling brings forth more exaggerated gestures and induces bouts of uncontrollable laughter. It is yet another story that strengthens our bond as it immortalizes the hunting adventures of my father and my brothers.

Chapter Twenty-Six
(Paternal) Grandpa Sam and Grandma Molly

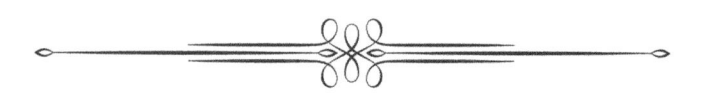

My siblings and I eagerly anticipated the arrival of summer each year, as it meant that sometimes we would have the opportunity to spend a cherished couple of weeks with our beloved Paternal Grandpa, Grandpa Sam, whom we affectionately called Papa. On Veterans Day 2022, I took to Facebook to pay tribute to this remarkable man who left a wonderful impression on our lives. Grandpa Sam's commitment to serving his country in the U.S. Army during both World Wars I and II demonstrated his extraordinary bravery, selflessness, hope, and love for his country.

When I reflect on Grandpa Sam's military service, I am sometimes overwhelmed with a wondrous sense of awe, gratitude, and pride. It is hard for me to fathom the challenges and hardships he must have endured as a soldier in those tumultuous times. The sacrifices he made and the dangers he faced on the front lines are unimaginable, but I believe that amid the chaos and uncertainty, he held onto a strong sense of purpose and his faith in God.

While I can never truly comprehend the depth of his experiences, I like to envision Grandpa Sam as a man who found comfort and strength in the belief that his actions were contributing to a greater cause. I imagine that even in the darkest moments, he must have held onto a steadfast pride in his mission, knowing that he was defending the values and freedoms that define our nation, even if those freedoms were a long time coming for our people.

Grandpa Sam's military service not only shaped his own life, but it also left a sense of pride and patriotism among our family. He fought in Europe at the same time as the famed Harlem Hell Fighters of the 369th Regiment. In my heart, judging by the strength and discipline of my father and my brothers, the Gibson men in general, I believe he was right there with the 369th. Could we ever trust them to let us know? Papa's service also inspired four of his great grandsons to serve. We learned the importance of honoring those who have served and sacrificed, recognizing that their contributions have paved the way for the liberties we cherish today. As I penned my tribute to Grandpa Sam on that Veterans Day, I felt an overwhelming sense of pride and admiration for him. Grandpa Sam's legacy will forever endure.

A Veritable Feast

My mother always made sure to nourish us abundantly before our eagerly anticipated summertime visit with Grandpa Sam and Grandma Molly. The anticipation filled our hearts with excitement as we approached their doorstep. As soon as we crossed the threshold, Grandma Molly would greet us with infectious enthusiasm, beckoning us inside. She would say, "Come on in here and eat! I know you must be famished. Your mama probably didn't have time to feed you properly. So come on in here and fill up those little bellies of yours."

However, the truth was that my mother took great care to ensure we were well-fed before she entrusted us to Grandpa Sam and Grandma Molly's care. She never failed to make sure we had enough to eat. Yet it seemed to bring Grandma Molly a peculiar sense of delight to take a jab at my mother. She insisted that Mama had neglected to feed us, even though it was far from reality. We would protest and inform Grandma Molly that we had already eaten, but our words fell on deaf ears. Undeterred, she would seat us at her table and lavish us with a veritable feast.

The centerpiece of this culinary delight was the most divine chicken smothered in a delectable gravy that remains unmatched by any I have ever tasted in my whole life! Its tantalizing aroma alone could make your tastebuds dance. Every bite I took was a symphony of flavors that tantalized the senses and left a lasting impression on my palate. The gravy was a showstopper; it was a blend of savory notes that melded together in perfect harmony. To this day, I have never encountered a gravy that could rival its extraordinary taste.

In addition to the mouthwatering chicken, Grandma Molly would grace our plates with a pile of biscuits, dripping with syrup, which created a heavenly combination of sweet and savory. She spared absolutely nothing in ensuring we were fully satiated, going above and beyond to indulge our appetites. We would devour this sumptuous feast and we were powerless to resist the temptation of the incredible flavors. As we continued to savor each morsel, our bellies gradually reached their limits, and the sensation of fullness washed over us. Unforgettable.

When the time came to bid farewell to Grandma Molly's table, we were completely and utterly stuffed. We still carry with us the memories of her culinary prowess, her ability to transform simple ingredients into masterpieces. The delicious food she so lovingly prepared for us forever holds a special place in our hearts, notwithstanding the digs she would take at our poor mother.

Goodbye Tokens

As summer drew to a close, bidding farewell to our cherished visits became an inevitable part of the routine, and Grandma Molly's heartfelt goodbyes added a touch of warmth to our parting moments. She would gather us together and line us up one by one to offer her personal farewell. As we embarked on our journey home, there was always an element of anticipation, for we knew that Grandma Molly's thoughtful gesture awaited us.

Among the traditions that had taken root over the years, Grandma Molly would handpick a single child to receive a treasured buffalo nickel. This small but valuable token held a special significance that was such an important part of those bygone days. In an era where such a coin held the genuine purchasing power of five cents, a small fortune to us, it opened the gateway to a world of delights—ice cream treats and an array of sugary candies that we savored. That buffalo nickel represented for us Grandma Molly's love, affection, and generosity, and it became a symbol of the joy and sweetness that her presence brought into our lives during those summer visits.

Grandma Molly's Jealousy

Grandpa Sam found himself navigating a precarious balance in his relationship with Grandma Molly. Her watchful eyes seemed to catch every subtle nod, friendly grin, or kind gesture he extended to any woman in their vicinity.

No small interaction went unnoticed by Grandma Molly's sharp gaze, and rather than sit in silent observation, Grandma Molly would unleash her accusations and berate Grandpa Sam with vexation. It seemed as if a storm brewed beneath the surface of their otherwise peaceful existence. Something was up.

Even when Grandpa Sam sought to distance himself to find solace on the porch, hoping to enjoy a moment of tranquility, Grandma Molly would emerge, her demeanor tense and accusatory. She would demand to know who he was gazing at, insinuating that his sole purpose for being out there was to steal glances at other women. Though none of us ever witnessed Grandpa casting his eyes inappropriately, Grandma Molly's persistent complaint always revolved around his alleged roving gaze. In her frustration, she would even threaten to fetch her gun. The target of her hypothetical shots remained unclear, but the message was crystal clear—Grandpa Sam had better watch his step. His loyalty was being questioned and Grandma Molly wasn't joking around.

Despite the persistent accusations against him, Grandpa Sam rarely engaged in a lengthy defense of himself. He seemed resigned to the routine and chose instead to listen in silence as Grandma Molly's unfounded accusations rang through the air for everyone to hear. It was as though he had grown accustomed to these episodes, and he accepted them as part of the fabric of his marriage to Grandma Molly.

Occasionally though, his exasperation would bubble over, and in those moments, all he would utter was a heartfelt, "Aww, Molly!" That simple phrase conveyed his weariness, his longing for her to cease and desist, and perhaps even a touch of mild amusement at the absurdity of the situation.

Their dynamic was one of contrasts—the tender moments of shared history and love of family and the overwhelming weight of mistrust. Through it all, Grandpa Sam weathered the storm of the accusations. I think he understood that sometimes the loudest protests were born from the deepest fears, and he chose to meet Grandma Molly's outbursts with patience and understanding.

Their relationship, fraught with jealousy and suspicion, was a study in the complexities of the human connection. In the midst of these turbulent episodes, love endured, albeit with occasional cracks. It was a love that had weathered countless storms but somehow always emerged intact.

Chapter Twenty-Seven
Aunt Fanny

I look back in amazement at Aunt Fannie. How did she always manage to have enough food for us, even when we showed up uninvited? Especially when there were already three sets of children living in her household.

She was my grandfather's sister, my grandmother's sister-in-law, and she was a wonderful woman. We loved her because she treated my siblings and I as if we were her own children. She always made us feel welcome in her home, and I can still feel the warmth and comfort that resonated throughout her entire house. It always just felt so good to be in her house.

Butter beans and peas galore, and they were always beyond delicious. Maybe the children of today wouldn't find this so incredible, but back then you ate what was set before you or you didn't eat at all. It just so happened that everything Aunt Fannie put before us was mouthwatering and delicious.

Her bread was not just any old plain bread. She baked it in a cast-iron skillet, and it seemed to rise to the height of a double- or triple-layer cake. It was every bit as delicious as cake, and we always tore it up. To sit at her table was a treat and we always ate everything she put before us. She welcomed us with open arms, and that's something a child is likely to never forget.

Aunt Fanny's grandchildren, her daughter's children, were just a few years older than we were, and we all went to the same school. Aunt Fanny's daughter's children included a set of twins, a girl and a boy. The boy was like a big brother. He would use my father's car to go see his girlfriend and take us with him.

Although they got off the bus before we did after school, we would somehow beat them to their own house and be sitting at the table waiting for one of Aunt Fanny's delicious meals before they changed out of their school clothes.

Around that table sat Aunt Fanny's children, her daughter's children, her son's children, and then us. This was never frowned upon or looked down on. We were always genuinely welcome by her, and it was completely normal for us to eat there.

I remember fighting with one of the boys over the last piece of bread. It was so delicious I wanted it for myself, but he had the same idea. Her son became exasperated at my liberty with the bread and said "Y'all should go home!" Aunt Fanny overheard the commotion and came in and divided the bread between us, giving me a larger share.

Aunt Fanny's house was fenced in and there was plenty of land around the house. Her granddaughters, Elizabeth and Hannah, were athletes. Hannah was our babysitter and stayed with us when our parents went out. She treated us all the same and was like a mother to us. She taught me what fairness was. They played on the basketball team in high school. We marveled and delighted at their athleticism when one of the girls would jump over the fence in the yard. We would watch her jump over the fence, clap thunderously, and ask her to do it over and over again. We were thrilled each time she jumped. Such simple pleasures. We remain friends with them to this day.

Aside from creating a welcoming, inviting home for visitors and preparing the best meals, Aunt Fanny had another talent. She could sew the fanciest clothes. Money was in limited supply in those days, but Aunt Fanny was resourceful. She utilized the sacks that the flour and animal feed came in to create some of the most beautiful dresses I had ever seen. She even embroidered flowers onto them, making the dresses the epitome of fashion for the day. I would sit and watch her sew. Her hands worked magic in my mind as they guided the fabric and threaded the needles. It was a thrill for me to watch her turn empty sacks into such beautiful clothes that I was always very proud to wear.

Sometimes she would let me press the machine pedal while she guided the fabric. She never used patterns to make the clothes. She never needed them. She had an innate talent for sewing and I was so lucky to be able to wear her beautiful, fashionable designs. Thank you, Aunt Fanny. I will never forget the love and kindness you showed me.

Chapter Twenty-Eight
Lola's Sweaters

Growing up in a sharecropping family meant that luxuries were few and far between. As I entered my teenage years, I started to notice the allure of fashionable clothes, jewelry, and other girly trinkets. However, with limited financial resources, acquiring those items seemed like an impossible dream. But as they say, necessity is the mother of invention, and I found a solution in the form of borrowing clothes from my friends.

Among my circle of friends, Lola Fox stood out for her impeccable sense of fashion. She had an uncanny ability to select the most stylish and trendy pieces, even on a limited budget. One day, Lola stumbled upon a sale and discovered two stunning sweaters. One was a rich burgundy color, while the other was a beautiful tan color. Instantly, I fell in love with both of them.

Lola, being the generous soul she was, allowed me to borrow the tan sweater. As soon as I put it on, it was as if magic enveloped me. The color complemented my complexion perfectly, and the fit was impeccable. I felt like a million bucks. With my limited wardrobe, I began to experiment, styling the tan sweater with every piece I owned. It became my go-to item, the centerpiece of my outfits.

I wore that sweater so much that people started associating it with me. When Lola would wear the sweater, people would say

"That's Mary Ann's sweater!" Little did they know that it actually belonged to Lola. Despite her temptation to set the record straight, she remained silent. She understood how much joy that sweater brought me, how it made me feel confident and beautiful. Lola kept my secret, allowing me to bask in its admiration and ownership.

Time passed, and eventually, I returned the sweater to Lola. She graciously accepted it back, and the next time I saw her, she was wearing it herself. People would still approach her, pointing out the sweater and attributing it to me. Lola never corrected them, choosing to keep our little secret intact. She had seen the genuine happiness that sweater brought me, and her selfless act of letting me keep it meant the world to me.

I'll forever be grateful to Lola for her kindness and understanding. She dubbed me "a little heifer" as she handed the sweater back to me, allowing me to cherish it as if it were truly mine. That tan sweater was a symbol of our friendship and the bond we formed. Thank you, Lola, for being a true friend and for making me feel like a fashion queen, even if it was just for a little while.

Chapter Twenty-Nine
Grandma Gertrude, Moonshine, and Big Joe

At one point in her life, my maternal grandmother, Grandma Gertrude, developed a fondness for alcohol. To put it mildly, she enjoyed indulging in excessive drinking. She had a mean streak when she was drinking, and she never hesitated to unleash her sharp tongue on anyone she believed deserved it. During a period when my children, Catherine and Andrew, were young, we all lived with Grandma Gertrude.

She remained unapproachable and maintained her mean-spirited demeanor throughout. Being well aware of her tendencies toward drink, her husband Big Joe would go to great lengths to hide his liquor from her, knowing all too well how she would overindulge if she found it.

However, Grandma Gertrude had a cunning ability to uncover Big Joe's secret hiding places. She would enlist the help of us children who worked out in the fields. Our job was to keep a close eye on Big Joe's actions and inform Grandma Gertrude whenever he came out to conceal his stash. When Big Joe was away, Grandma would provide us with a jar and instruct us to retrieve the moonshine from its secret spot and bring it to her.

We also had the responsibility of replacing the stolen moonshine with water, giving the mixture a thorough shake to make sure Big Joe remained oblivious to the fact that his cherished liquor had been looted. We left no trace of our deceit. Big Joe would return home, only to discover Grandma Gertrude totally inebriated. It was when Big Joe flexed his entrepreneurial muscles that he found out that his moonshine had been tampered with. Little did he know that it was us children who had aided and abetted Grandma Gertrude, serving as her accomplices in this operation.

She loved moonshine and occasional drunkenness, but Grandma Gertrude did not allow her habit to interfere with her job. She was employed to care for the children of a White family, and in their eyes, she was cherished and adored. The family held Grandma Gertrude in high regard, showered her with love and praise, and were always ready to offer any assistance she might need.

The underlying reasons behind Grandma's meanness and her affinity for moonshine remained a mystery to us. However, one day, without warning, she made a sudden decision to quit drinking. The allure of getting drunk no longer held any significance for her. With this change, Grandma Gertrude became slightly kinder and more amicable, a shift that didn't go unnoticed by those around her.

Big Joe was delighted by the remarkable transformation in Grandma Gertrude. He showed his appreciation by purchasing her a car, a Gran Prix. Despite Grandma Gertrude never having learned how to drive, Big Joe wanted her to enjoy the luxury and independence of having her own vehicle. Her driving escapades were far from graceful, though. She ran into and over garbage cans, bumped into wooden fences, and caused havoc in the streets when she got behind the wheel. But regardless of the damages Grandma Gertrude incurred with her reckless driving, the caring White family she worked for always stepped in to address any damages. They held a deep affection for her, readily taking responsibility for repairing any accidents or mishaps Grandma Gertrude caused. They took exceptional care to see that she had everything she needed.

The fact that Grandma Gertrude miraculously stopped drinking was truly astonishing. Along with her newfound sobriety, she even developed a regular habit of attending church, and the White family she worked for bought her a complete, new wardrobe.

On a particular Sunday, she went to church with extraordinary devotion. She testified, danced, and praised God with every fiber of her being. She expressed her readiness to be taken by God at that very moment if it was His will. However, there was one heartfelt desire she wished to fulfill before her departure: to see her son Robbie, who happened to be my favorite uncle. Unfortunately, Robbie, who was involved in the earlier incident I mentioned about the bulldozer, was absent from church that Sunday. Still, Grandma's final request on this earthly plane was for her Robbie's presence.

After several minutes of fervent singing, shouting, dancing, and praising God, Grandma Gertrude, who was in good health and had even driven herself to church that day, found a moment of respite. She sat down after worshipping God to the fullest, leaning her head on the shoulder of the woman sitting beside her, and passed away peacefully. Some people thought that Grandma Gertrude was simply resting from her high-spirited worship, but in reality, she was taking her last breaths on earth. When I was an undergraduate student, this sad turn of events led me to write an essay about my grandmother Gertrude's last day on earth.

Chapter Thirty
Early Career and Casey's Support

From the very beginning, when I toiled in the fields as a young girl under the hot and unforgiving Georgia sun alongside my sharecropper parents, the desire to become a teacher burned deep within me. The sight of my parents' determination and hard work instilled in me a profound appreciation for the transformative power of education. The allure of teaching became more and more irresistible to me. I had always held teachers in the highest regard, and in my eyes, they embodied the essence of nobility and dignity. I deeply admired the work they did.

I wanted to garner for myself the kind of respect and appreciation that seemed to my young eyes to be bestowed upon every teacher that I knew.

It never escaped me, however, that picking peaches and cotton in the fields of rural Georgia was a far cry from being in front of a classroom molding young minds. Still, I had my dreams, and fortunately for me, I was raised to believe that with effort, persistence, and prayer, dreams could sometimes come true.

To have the privilege of guiding and helping to develop impressionable minds, teaching them to decipher the intricacies of written words and the logic behind numbers, was a calling I could not ignore. The prospect of witnessing the flicker of understanding in a student's eyes, that moment when the door of comprehension swung wide open, was a reward beyond measure. My heart swelled with anticipation at the mere thought of kindling that spark within students under my tutelage.

The notion of teaching captivated my imagination and set it ablaze with endless possibilities. Being a teacher wasn't just a career choice; it was my heart yearning to make a positive impact on people's lives. I longed to guide young people on their educational journeys and to offer assistance and support along the way. My aspirations as an educator extended beyond the confines of the classroom; I wanted my teachings to resonate with my students long after they had grown into adulthood. My classroom methods of problem-solving resonated with my students because I involved them in the process. They relished the many occasions where we held courtlike proceedings and debates to determine the best approaches to remedy their issues. Our proceedings extended beyond typical classroom issues and encompassed everything from their dating dilemmas to their classroom conflicts. They trusted me with their problems. They knew that I would allow them the freedom to express themselves and that they would be heard. They knew their voices and concerns always mattered in Ms. Gibson's room, and they loved me for that.

I envisioned myself as not only an educator but also a mentor, guiding them along the pathways of their individual journeys. I wanted to instill not just knowledge, but also confidence, resilience, and empathy in their hearts. It was my belief that education was not confined to the walls of a classroom; it was a transformative force that could shape the course of one's existence.

As I delved deeper into the art of teaching, I recognized the profound responsibility that rested upon my shoulders. I understood that the influence I wielded had the potential to reverberate throughout the lives of my students long after they left the sanctuary of my classroom. It was a weighty realization, one that ignited a dedication within me. I vowed to be not only an instructor of subject matter, but also a source of inspiration and guidance, and to mold young minds with love, patience, and support.

As the years passed I stood at the helm of countless classrooms, witnessing the growth and evolution of my students. I reveled in their accomplishments, celebrating not only their academic triumphs but also the personal milestones they achieved. And with every success story, my sense of fulfillment deepened, knowing that I had played a role, however small, in shaping their lives. These ideals became an integral part of my legacy as a teacher, and I approached my work with the utmost dedication and seriousness.

I had one student, a young boy who seemed to only come to school to get into trouble. He never stopped being mischievous. It's like he had a personal mission to turn my hair gray before retirement. If there was a Guinness World Record for being told, "Quiet down and take your seat" in a single school year, he would be the undisputed champion.

So one day, in a moment of sheer exasperation, I summoned all my teacher authority, grabbed a pointer, and told him, "Enough is enough! Follow me outside the classroom, young man."

Now, I have to confess, the thought of paddling a student had never crossed my mind before. My classrooms had been paddle-free my whole career, and I couldn't help but feel a tad bit nervous about the whole affair. I mean, would I paddle too hard? Too soft? What if I hurt the poor thing?

As we made our way outside, both he and I wore expressions of trepidation. I told him to assume the position, which meant for him to put his hands up and lean against the wall. With pointer in hand, I tentatively approached. The suspense was palpable, almost like a scene from an intense action movie, except the action was confined to a school hallway without an audience.

With trembling hands and a trembling heart, I mustered all my courage and went for the tap—just a light tap, mind you. But alas, the pointer was no match for my tenderhearted nature. I burst into tears.

To my surprise, the mischievous rascal came to my aid. He put his arm around my shoulder and provided a comforting gesture that melted my heart even more. In a voice as soothing as melted chocolate, he uttered those unforgettable words: "Miss Gibson, don't cry. I get a whipping at home every day. This was nothing. Don't cry! My momma whip me every day!" Now, I have to admit, we were quite the sight—a rebellious student comforting a weeping teacher. I composed myself, wiped away my tears, and together we reentered the classroom. As we entered the classroom, the students saw me crying and demanded of him, "What did you do to Ms. Gibson?" That student is a young man now with a family of his own. Today, when I see him out in the community from time to time, he jokingly puts his hands up like he's leaning against the wall awaiting his paddling, and we share the biggest laugh over the memory of that incident we created so many years ago. Sometimes the best lessons we teach aren't found in textbooks or in detentions and punishments, but in those unexpected moments of compassion and unlikely friendships.

Today, as I reflect upon my journey, I am filled with gratitude for the privilege of being a teacher. The impact I have made, the lives I have touched, and the legacy I have forged have surpassed my wildest dreams. The path was not always smooth, but the passion that burned within me propelled me forward. Now, I can most assuredly say that I did my job, and I did it well. So say many of my students to this day, where most of them are grown up with families of their own.

Casey's Support

When I completed my student teacher program, I was surprised to discover that there was a dress code at Fort Valley State University. However, the rule posed a challenge for me as it strictly prohibited wearing slacks and mandated dresses or skirts instead. Unfortunately,

I didn't own any suitable attire to meet this requirement. It was a busy and exciting time for me, but I was so fortunate to have friends like Gail and Nell who were kind and fully supportive of my new career. They taught me how to sew so that I could begin to make my own clothes. Gail, my guardian angel, taught me to sew for myself and for my children. When I started teaching, she also designed and sewed a new wardrobe for me at her own expense. She would cook the most delicious meals and our children played together as we sewed. Also, as fate would have it, I had another extraordinary friend who came to my immediate rescue: Casey, another guardian angel. Casey selflessly offered her assistance and provided me with the fabric needed to create an entirely new wardrobe for my budding teaching career. She didn't charge me a penny and took it upon herself to craft beautiful garments that would not only meet the dress code but also exude elegance and style. Casey's impeccable craftsmanship and attention to detail made each piece a fashion statement.

People couldn't help but notice my fashionable attire and would often inquire where I had purchased such fine clothes. With immense pride, I would explain that they were not store-bought, but instead lovingly crafted by my dear friend, Casey.

But Casey's support extended far beyond fashion. She went above and beyond by offering encouragement and even typing my academic papers. I credit her with not only assisting me during my student teaching days but also with directly helping me earn both my bachelor's and master's degrees.

Casey was my steadfast companion, guiding me through every step of my educational journey, and for that, I will be forever grateful.

I am eternally thankful to Gail, Casey, and Nell for the divine spark within them that consistently uplifted and sustained me. They are truly the most remarkable people I have had the privilege to know. Their generosity, talent, and unfailing support will always hold a special place in my heart, and I will never forget their invaluable contributions to my success. May you, the person reading this book, also find incredible friends like Gail, Casey, and Nell who fully support your endeavors, who bring light, love, and inspiration to your life's path.

Chapter Thirty-One
A Janitor, a Maid

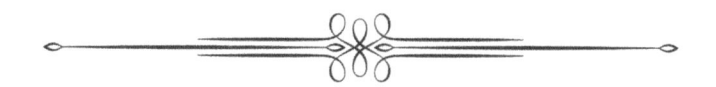

In one of my first forays into the working world, I took a position as a maid and a janitor at a school in my county. In my experience, it was the teachers and the principal who looked down their noses at me, as if I wasn't worthy of respect because of the kind of work I did. Rarely if ever was I subjected to this kind of reaction by the students. Regardless of the job title, I have always held the belief that one should strive to perform their duties to the best of their abilities. My work ethic was formed as I observed and worked with my parents both at home and in the fields. I carried this principle with me into my job as a cleaner, and I was not ashamed. I took great pride in my work as I meticulously maintained the cleanliness of the halls and bathrooms under my responsibility. In most schools, the teachers' facilities are usually separate from those used by students. Remarkably, the bathrooms I maintained for students were so immaculate that the teachers chose to utilize them rather than their own designated restrooms.

When I saw students in the hallways from time to time, I would always encourage them all to do their very best in school and to be on their best behavior. I told them that they were smart, and to always let their teachers know just how smart they were. I explained the consequences to them of not doing their best on class exams. I told them that if they didn't do their best to pass their exams, that they were in jeopardy of being retained for the following year. I explained to them that that meant their friends would move on to the next higher grade, while they themselves would be left behind to repeat the same grade the next year.

I elaborated on the significance of maintaining cleanliness in the classrooms to the students. I highlighted the importance of not throwing paper on the floor, even when they were outside. I conveyed to them that having clean classrooms daily would make them proud, and it would reflect positively if the superintendent or even the President of the United States were to visit.

If I witnessed a fight or if I happened to see a fight beginning to start, I would intervene. I would tell the students involved that no matter who hit first, they would both be in trouble because those were the rules. I gave them a choice: I could either tell the teacher about the fight, or I could just tell her to have a word with the students without providing the teacher with all the details. Although most of the students listened to me and exhibited good behavior, there were one or two who were unruly. These particular students would run fast down the hallway and then slide on their knees. They thought this was fun, but it was a bit dangerous. One day, the mother of one of these students visited the school and witnessed firsthand her son sliding down the hallway. She chastised her son and told him, "If Miss Gibson tells you to stop doing something, then you better stop doing it right then and there." This gave me a great deal of satisfaction because it meant that everyone knew I had the students' best interests at heart.

During the holidays, I received so many presents from students. I took this as a sign that they knew I cared about them. My godson Stan, who I am so very proud of, happened to be a student at that time, and to this day he thanks me for my advice. He always did only enough to get by, but I told him how smart he was. I recognized his abilities and pushed him to do more.

Chapter Thirty-Two
Help! Call the Police!

You know, I never did care much for driving. Perhaps this has something to do with my trauma from the first-grade last day of school bus accident that I mentioned earlier. I do know that I never liked being behind the wheel of a car much, and to this day I only drive when it's absolutely necessary.

As a matter of fact, when I was getting my doctorate degree, the school I attended was in another state, a seven hour drive down Interstate 75. I was never going to do that alone!

Although much of my coursework was online, one of the main requirements of my graduate program was that I had to attend class in person on several weekends of the semester. I wasn't happy with this arrangement, but I really wanted that doctorate degree.

One particular weekend I really just didn't want to go. Everything in me was against making that trip. I was nervous about being on the Interstate for over seven hours. In my mind, that was such a long span of time, and it seemed like there would be too much opportunity for something to go wrong. I was scared. No matter how much I hemmed and hawed, my family and friends encouraged me to go anyway. No, they insisted that I go. They suggested ways to help me relax during the trip. "Nothing's going to happen. It'll be a nice trip, a nice getaway for you. Listen to music. Take a sleeping pill. Read a book. Before you know it, you'll be there." Still, I did not want to go. Outside of the prospect of the long drive, I was unprepared because I hadn't fully completed my part of a group project that would be due upon arrival. I didn't want to go! Enter my beloved friend Mrs. Sandy, who without hesitation not only offered to drive me there, but to stay with me for the entire weekend of my course.

Casey was free with her time in that regard as well. She never minded driving whenever I had to go somewhere important. She never complained about the trip or gave me any indication that she was anything other than happy to drive for me, even the long distance to school. I love and appreciate Casey more than words can ever express.

I'm so glad that my friends and family convinced me to go for that weekend course. To my surprise, when I arrived, the professor put the class into groups and allowed us time to finish the project that was due upon arrival. I was partnered with a class colleague who happened to work for a state university in the very department that correlated with the course we were taking.

As it turned out, she had not completed the assignment either. But what is incredible is that the part of the assignment that she completed happened to be the very part that I never got around to finishing. We each had the missing pieces of the puzzle. We quickly put our unfinished assignments together and made a full, incredible presentation, for which we received the highest grade. I am so glad that I made the trip for my course that weekend, my initial apprehension notwithstanding.

As the years went on, my colleague became a very close friend, and to this day we enjoy the best sisterly relationship.

Another thing I remember about Casey driving me around is that once we were driving somewhere, engrossed in conversation that had us both laughing uncontrollably. In the midst of that, Casey inadvertently hit the curb slightly. It was nothing to hurt either of us, but it gave me a momentary fright. A surge of emotion overcame me, causing me to blurt out, "Watch where you're going. Don't you go off the damn road again!" My exaggerated hysteria made Casey laugh even harder. I told her, "You think I'm joking? Don't go off that damn road again. Do it and I'll beat your ass right here and right now. You think I'm playing, you just try me! I will beat your whole ass!" My increasing intensity and tirade of threats of violence only made Casey laugh harder.

As we pulled into a drive-through restaurant for a bite to eat, I was still going on and on about her hitting the curb. The intensity and passion in my voice had not decreased. I was still in anger mode and my tone was confrontational. My demeanor was so exaggerated that the restaurant employees heard me through their microphones. Concerned over what they were hearing, they all huddled together at the payment window to check on Casey's well-being, to see if she needed help. "Ma'am, are you okay? Do you need help? Can we call the police for you?" They were going to call the police because they thought she needed protection from me because of my tone and my passionate threats toward her. As the seriousness of the employees' concern dawned on Casey, she couldn't help but burst into laughter again. She reassured the concerned restaurant staff members. "No, I don't need any damned help! This is my friend I'm talking to. We're just having a conversation, and no I don't need any help! Thank you for your concern, though."

Casey and I have a shared understanding in our friendship, and we get boisterous with each other sometimes. We were struck by the realization that we were overheard by others who didn't know us, and that they thought she was in peril. We just couldn't contain our laughter.

Again though, as I reflect on this incident, it is clear to me that my passionate reaction to Casey bumping the curb was rooted in the deep fear and anxiety I developed after the bus accident long ago when I was in the first grade.

Chapter Thirty-Three
Twiggs County and Professional Challenges

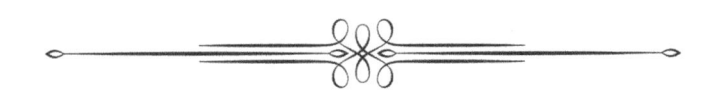

I consider myself extremely fortunate to have completed my undergraduate studies ahead of schedule. During the pursuit of my master's degree, an incredible opportunity came my way: a teaching position in the heart of Twiggs County, Georgia, at a school known as Dry Branch Georgia. Embracing this chance, I eagerly accepted the role and found myself teaching sixth-grade students.

From the very beginning, it was evident that a deep connection was forming between my students and me. They quickly became enamored with my teaching style, and I, in turn, became deeply attached to their unique personalities and their thirst for knowledge.

My time at Dry Branch Georgia was life-changing. Every day, as I walked through the school doors, I was greeted by the sheer enthusiasm and eagerness for learning that emanated from my students. The classroom was filled with laughter, inquisitive minds, and the pursuit of learning and growth. Witnessing their progress and seeing their faces light up with understanding brought me immense joy and a sense of fulfillment.

However, despite the profound bond I had developed with my students and the immeasurable support from the dedicated principal,

Mr. Warring, fate had other plans in store for me. An opportunity presented itself, beckoning me back to my hometown, and I couldn't resist the call. With a mix of excitement and nostalgia, I bid farewell to the cherished memories and relationships I had formed at Dry Branch Georgia and embarked on a new chapter in my teaching career.

Returning to my hometown to teach was a decision that filled me with great anticipation. It allowed me to reconnect with the place that had shaped my formative years and with students who shared a common background and experiences. The warmth and familiarity of my hometown resonated within the school's walls, creating an environment that fostered growth and togetherness. The school's supportive community, coupled with the inspiring leadership of Mr. Warring, fueled my passion for teaching, reinforcing my belief in the transformative power of education.

Although my time teaching in my hometown was undeniably brief, it left a lasting mark on my professional journey. The relationships I forged with my students were profound and memorable, instilling in me a deep appreciation for the impact educators can have on young lives. The guidance and encouragement provided by Mr. Warring further solidified my commitment to nurturing the potential of every student who crossed my path.

Reflecting upon my experiences at Dry Branch Georgia and my subsequent return to my hometown, I realize that each chapter in my teaching career has contributed to my growth as an educator. The challenges and joys, the connections and farewells, all shaped me into the passionate and dedicated teacher I had become over the years.

I carry with me the memories and lessons from my time in both Dry Branch Georgia and my hometown, serving as a constant reminder of the profound impact teachers can have and the immense privilege it is to be part of a student's journey.

A Career Highlight

One of the most memorable milestones in my professional life was undoubtedly winning the highly esteemed Teacher of the Year award. What made this achievement even more exceptional was the fact that it was based on the votes of my students, rather than my colleagues, and I accomplished this feat during my very first year as an educator. To my sheer delight, I was even fortunate enough to be bestowed with this honor a second time.

The students who cast their votes for me were ranged from fifth to eighth graders, and I firmly believe that their choice was largely influenced by the genuine love and compassion I effortlessly shared with them, which they, in turn, reciprocated. Their acceptance of me as their teacher, coupled with their remarkable academic progress resulting from my teaching methods, served as an extraordinary confidence booster for a young, aspiring educator. They unequivocally affirmed my decision to pursue a career in education and, unbeknownst to them, they silently assisted me in defying all the doubters who said that I would never amount to anything. How wrong they were! I not only proved them wrong then, but I continued to thrive as an accomplished teacher even in the face of professional adversity.

Regrettably, the subsequent years saw a change in policy, whereby students were no longer able to participate in the voting process for this prestigious award of Teacher of the Year. Instead, the responsibility fell upon the teachers themselves to select the recipient. Following the implementation of this new policy, I never had the privilege of receiving the award again for the remainder of my career.

Although it was disheartening to no longer be recognized with this honor, I refused to let it diminish the impact I had on my students' lives and the fulfillment I found in shaping their educational journeys. The memories of their support and the profound difference I made in their lives will forever hold a special place in my heart.

In retrospect, winning the Teacher of the Year award based on student votes remains a cherished highlight in my professional trajectory. It not only validated my choice to pursue teaching but also instilled in me the confidence and determination to excel regardless of the challenges I faced. While the subsequent policy change denied me the opportunity to receive the award again, I take solace in knowing that my true measure of success was forged in the positive impact I had on countless students throughout my career.

Professional Challenges

The tides of change were undeniably in motion. You see, later that year, a new superintendent assumed the helm, and unfortunately, things took a rapid downturn. I found myself in her crosshairs, seemingly the target of her disapproval, incapable of doing anything right in her discerning eyes.

It can be immensely challenging when someone harbors animosity toward you, leaving you with limited options to resolve their grievances. However, I was resolute in my determination to persist. I had invested countless hours studying diligently and working tirelessly to become a teacher, making it my dream profession. As Esther aptly conveyed to Grady in an episode of *Sanford and Son*, "I'm here, and I'm staying here!"

On one ill-fated day, I encountered a severe setback. I unexpectedly tumbled down a treacherous flight of nine iron steps, inflicting a significant injury to my back. Little did I know at the time that the maintenance worker had recently waxed the steps, without placing any warning signs in sight. Realizing the need to protect my interests, I engaged the services of an attorney.

As a consequence, the following year saw me transferred to another school, a decision likely influenced by the superintendent's unfavorable opinion of me. Regrettably, the reception from my new principal mirrored the superintendent's sentiment. Although a few colleagues treated me with similar coldness, I was fortunate to find a modicum of respect and professional courtesy from the curriculum director, who happened to be the principal's wife. The path before me was arduous and full of challenges. I became subject to cold and isolating treatments. It was as if they were determined to send me a clear message that I had no place within their ranks.

The emotional toll was immense; I experienced profound hurt and anger and shed countless tears. Nonetheless, I persevered for a few more years, weathering the storm of the negativity, hostility, and plain ugliness that surrounded me. I had a family to support and responsibilities to fulfill, and above all, I held a deep love for the art of teaching. Still, I am human, and the relentless isolation and maltreatment inflicted upon me by my colleagues eventually became unbearable.

The volatile conditions under which I toiled showed no signs of improvement, leaving me with no choice but to make a difficult decision. I decided enough was enough. I chose to leave, to uproot myself and seek solace elsewhere. I relocated and found a new haven in Warner Robins, Georgia. Miraculously, in the same year of my move, a job opportunity arose at a local elementary school, an opportunity for which I am eternally grateful to a higher power. I yearned for a fresh start in my professional life, and this newfound prospect before me was an unequivocal blessing.

The transition to my new teaching position brought with it a renewed sense of hope and optimism.

I felt a renewed passion for my craft as I embraced the chance to make a positive impact on the lives of young learners.

The challenges I faced in my previous chapter undoubtedly shaped me, fostering resilience and fortitude. They served as a reminder of the importance of finding an environment that values and appreciates one's contributions. The move to Warner Robins, Georgia, marked a turning point in my professional journey, where I could finally channel my passion for teaching into a positive and fulfilling experience.

Chapter Thirty-Four
Educational Philosophy

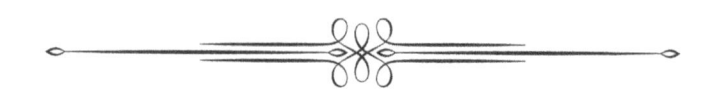

Teaching has always been both natural and fulfilling for me. I wholeheartedly believe it to be the most rewarding career choice I could have ever made. From the beginning, I recognized and understood the major impact that the learning environment and climate have on the growth and development of young minds. In my educational philosophy, I placed great emphasis on creating the ideal conditions for children to thrive both academically and personally. This meant that I took it as my responsibility to ensure their safety, to foster their trust in me as an educator, to nurture a sense of respect, and to recognize the inherent humanity and dignity of each child.

With these fundamental principles in mind, I dedicated myself to creating an optimal learning environment for my students, whom I lovingly referred to as my children. I sought to establish a climate of care, understanding, and mutual respect, where every individual felt valued and supported.

I'm happy to say that my children understood these principles, and what's even more worthy of note is that they not only demonstrated these principles among each other, they extended them to me as well.

For example, once when I was working at a middle school, I wasn't having the best day. Earlier, I had been summoned to the principal's office. There was a meeting wherein I was accused of something that I did not do. What's worse is that the principal knew I was innocent, but that didn't seem to matter to him. He went through with the charade of reprimand, knowing how it would devastate me, knowing that I was innocent, and knowing that he was abusing his authority in such a meaningless and despicable way. The whole experience was a bit harrowing and left me feeling a bit stung. I wasn't myself for the rest of the day. I needed a hug and to hear "I love you" from someone. The end of the day finally arrived, and the bus riders were called to go to their buses. One student, Bon Bon, walked by me and said, "Goodbye Ms. Gibson."

"Goodbye. I love you," came my reply. Immediately, she turned around and gave me a note. The note read, "I love you so much. You are special to me."

Bon Bon told me she didn't know why she wrote the note; she wrote it as soon as she got to school that morning, but she had forgotten to give it to me. But I knew why. Because of her kind gesture, a sense of peace enveloped me. I looked out the window and saw the sun shining brightly. In that moment, it was as if I saw the son of God at work. And then I cried. I was reminded and I understood that there are many ways to feel God's glory, and I felt loved.

Chapter Thirty-Five
The Not-So-Good Things About Teaching

For me, teaching was a calling. I knew this from my earliest days of sitting out in the dirt under the hot sun in my small, segregated, rural town playing school with my siblings and cousins.

Teaching wasn't just a profession for me; it was a deep-seated calling that manifested itself from my earliest memories. Growing up in a small, segregated, rural town, I spent countless hours playing school with my siblings and cousins. Our makeshift classrooms were nothing more than patches of dirt under the scorching sun.

It was in those humble settings that I discovered the innate joy of sharing knowledge even in its simplest form. It ignited a fire within me—a passion that would fuel my lifelong commitment to education.

As I grew older, my dedication to teaching solidified. I pursued higher education, immersing myself in pedagogical theories and instructional practices. I sought opportunities to observe and learn from seasoned educators who inspired me with their dedication, creativity, and ability to ignite a passion for learning in their students.

With each step on my educational journey, I gained a deeper understanding of the power of education to transform lives. I recognized the potential to shape not just minds but also hearts and souls. I realized that being a teacher meant being a guide, a mentor, and a champion for every learner who crossed my path.

I embraced the responsibility that came with my calling. I dedicated countless hours to crafting engaging lesson plans, tailoring my teaching methods to accommodate diverse learning styles, and fostering an inclusive and nurturing classroom environment. I strove to foster critical thinking, creativity, and a lifelong love for learning among my students. Their growth and success became my greatest reward.

Teaching, for me, was never just a job. It was a purposeful journey fueled by a burning desire to make a positive impact on the lives of others. It was about breaking down barriers, empowering young minds, and creating a more equitable and just society. Through education, I hoped to inspire future generations to dream big, believe in themselves, and reach their fullest potential.

As I reflect on my path, I realize that my humble beginnings playing school in the dirt under the hot sun were a foreshadowing of the meaningful and fulfilling career that awaited me. Teaching was not just a calling. It was my life's mission—a mission I would continue to embrace with passion and dedication.

What I imagined as a little girl about teaching and the reality I came to know of the profession as an adult did not always match my expectations. While I loved teaching, there was no way I could anticipate as a child the harsher realities of what that life would be.

I harbor no regrets regarding my career choice; however, I must acknowledge my honest sentiments. There were times when I yearned to pursue a profession other than teaching. Now that I have embarked on my retirement journey, I believe it is fitting to shed light on some of the less favorable aspects of teaching, as perceived through my own experience.

Despite the following challenges, I was a dedicated educator, and I still found pure joy and fulfillment in the noble task of shaping young minds:

1. Heavy Workload: As a teacher, I often faced a significant workload, including lesson-planning, grading papers, and preparing materials. This, on top of managing individual student progress, was sometimes overwhelming for me.
2. Administrative Responsibilities: Besides teaching, I was often burdened with administrative duties such as paperwork, record-keeping, and attending meetings. These additional responsibilities often took away valuable time that I wished could be spent on my instructional activities.
3. Classroom Management: Maintaining discipline and managing a classroom of energetic young students could be a real challenge at times. It was my responsibility to manage behavior issues, promote a positive learning environment, and cater to the diverse needs of my students simultaneously, not always an easy feat for one individual.
4. Limited Resources: There were times when budget constraints and lack of resources hindered the effectiveness of my teaching. There were times when I had to make do with limited supplies, outdated textbooks, and insufficient technology resources, which impacted my ability to provide the best learning experience for my students.
5. Parental Involvement: Collaborating with parents was and remains essential for a child's education, but it could also be a source of stress. Dealing with uncooperative parents, addressing concerns, and maintaining effective communication could often be time-consuming and emotionally draining.
6. Standardized Testing Pressure: The prevalence of standardized testing in education places additional pressure on teachers. There were times when I felt compelled to teach to the test

rather than focus on creative learning experiences. I resisted this temptation and opted instead to teach my children how to actually take tests.

I realized the importance of equipping my children with effective test-taking skills. It became clear to me that students who are taught these skills have a greater chance of excelling in any given test. Therefore, I made it a priority to teach them the art of deductive reasoning. Incorporating deductive reasoning into test-taking skills will empower your students to approach exams with a logical and methodical mindset. It will enhance their analytical thinking.

Chapter Thirty-Six
Support For New Teachers

My teaching career spanned the course of more than three decades. As I journey into a new chapter of my life, I would like to offer a few words of encouragement and a bit of advice for future teachers in their efforts to shape the minds of the next generation:

1. Embrace student individuality: As a teacher, I tried to do this as often as possible because I understood that every student is different. Each student has different learning styles, strengths, and challenges in learning. Appreciate their individuality and adapt your teaching strategies to cater to their diverse needs as often as possible. This was not always an easy thing to do, but I believe it to be a worthwhile endeavor for teachers to undertake because it creates an inclusive and empowering learning environment for students. When teachers embrace student individuality, they recognize that each student brings a unique set of skills, talents, and perspectives to the classroom. This will create for students a sense of belonging, as they feel seen and understood for who they truly are.

   When you include teaching strategies to accommodate the different needs of students whenever possible, you as a teacher engage students in the learning process. Some students may thrive in visual or auditory learning environments, while others may excel through hands-on activities or group discussions. My advice is to incorporate a variety of instructional methods to ensure that every student has the opportunity to succeed.

When you embrace their individuality, you cultivate a sense of self-confidence for your students. Encourage students to express their ideas and opinions and watch as they develop a stronger sense of self and become more willing to take risks in learning and understanding. I believe this also helps develop their critical thinking skills and supports their natural creativity.

When students see that their differences are appreciated, they are more likely to respect and celebrate the differences of their peers, leading to an atmosphere of mutual respect and empathy.

I think it is important to note that embracing student individuality is not just a challenging task for teachers; it is a transformative approach to education as a whole. This weight does not rest solely on the shoulders of teachers. By recognizing and appreciating the unique qualities of each student, adapting teaching strategies, and creating an inclusive learning environment, teachers can empower their students to reach their full potential.

2. Build meaningful relationships: Establishing positive relationships with your students is crucial. Take the time to understand them, show genuine care, and create a safe and supportive learning environment.
3. Foster inclusiveness: Emphasize the importance of inclusiveness and create an atmosphere where all students feel valued and respected, regardless of their background, abilities, or differences.
4. Be flexible and adaptable: Teaching is a dynamic profession, and flexibility is key. Be open to trying new approaches, adjusting your lesson plans, and accommodating unexpected changes to meet the evolving needs of your students. If you see that an

approach is not working, don't be afraid to adjust it or throw it out and create a new approach. Time is of utmost importance.

5. Encourage critical thinking: Foster critical thinking skills by providing opportunities for students to analyze, evaluate, and question information. I frequently held "court" in my classrooms and my students responded favorably by learning how to synthesize information. I encouraged them to think independently, solve problems, and express their opinions respectfully.

6. Maintain high expectations: Set high expectations for your students and believe in their potential. Challenge them to strive for excellence while providing the necessary support and guidance to help them succeed. Set a high bar, but never leave them alone, afraid, and/or unsure about how to reach the top.

7. Practice effective communication: Develop strong communication skills to effectively convey ideas, instructions, and feedback to your students. Actively listen to their concerns, address them promptly, and encourage open dialogue in the classroom.

8. Emphasize the process, not just the outcome: Focus on the learning process rather than solely emphasizing grades or results. Encourage perseverance, resilience, and a growth mindset, where mistakes are viewed as opportunities for growth and improvement.

9. Collaborate with colleagues: Seek opportunities to collaborate and learn from your fellow teachers. This may prove difficult at times due to personalities and/or other factors, but as much as possible, share ideas, resources, and strategies, and support each other in creating a positive educational experience for all students.

10. Practice self-care: Teaching can be demanding, both physically and emotionally. Prioritize self-care to avoid burnout and maintain your own well-being. Take time for yourself, engage in activities you enjoy, and seek support when needed.

Getting enough sleep is crucial for rejuvenation. Every day is a challenge and adequate sleep will equip you with the proper frame of mind to meet those challenges. Prioritize sleep by establishing a consistent sleep schedule. I further suggest creating a relaxing bedtime routine.

Take time out for activities you enjoy. This can provide you with a sense of fulfillment and relaxation. It can be anything from reading, painting, or gardening to playing a musical instrument or participating in sports.

As a teacher, you will find that community is vital. Building and nurturing meaningful relationships with friends, family, and colleagues is important for emotional well-being. Make time for socializing, whether it's meeting up with friends, phone conversations, joining a club or community group, or participating in online forums.

I would be remiss if I failed to include here the importance of establishing clear boundaries between your professional and personal lives. This is essential for preventing burnout. Learn to say no when necessary, delegate tasks, and create a work schedule that allows for personal time and relaxation.

It's important to reach out for support when you feel it is needed. Talk to trusted colleagues, friends, or family members about any challenges you're facing. Also, consider seeking professional help, such as counseling or therapy, to process emotions and develop coping strategies. It can work wonders.

Self-care is a very personal proposition, and it's important to find what works best for you. My advice is to tailor these examples to suit your needs and prioritize self-care as an integral part of your daily routine. Not only do I think you will benefit as a more effective teacher, but your general well-being will improve as well.

Chapter Thirty-Seven
Epilogue

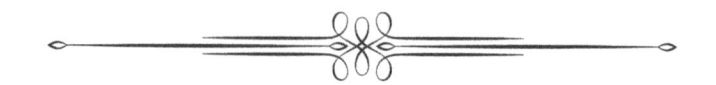

Throughout my three-plus decades of teaching, it was my pleasure to collaborate with, to support, and to encourage my children. The close bond I forged with them provided me with insight to their lives and their experiences. I therefore became attuned to the signs of trouble brewing at home. I became familiar with their struggles, difficulties, and hardships. At the same time, I became acquainted with their aspirations and dreams. Observing their resilience and diligence, I also witnessed their triumphant moments and provided support to them during challenging times. Above all, my utmost aspiration was to enrich their lives with enlightenment, empowerment, joy, and happiness during the hours they spent under my care and guidance.

In my retirement, I am filled with an overwhelming sense of delight and joy as I discover that numerous students, who have now embarked on their own careers and started their own families, still hold memories of me close to their hearts. I am proud to know that many of my former students are doing so well and are active in the community as teachers, parents, law enforcement officers, small business owners, medical professionals, members of the armed forces, and many other rewarding careers. Their continued admiration and kind words about the impact I had on their lives uplifts me every day. When they found out that I was writing this book, this is the kindness and support they offered me, and I am grateful to each and every one of them, to all my former students—near and far. Following are some very kind words about me that a few of my children wanted to share about their experiences with me as their teacher.

You are my maternal grace and mercy and I am fortunate to have such an inestimable presence in our lives. Yahweh loves me and my children so much that he created you and shared you with us as the loving, educated, charismatic, amiable, comedic, devout, true hearted, selfless, inspiring, resolute, discerning, spiritual guru and mentor that you are. I humbly thank you and appreciate your existence. Forever grateful.

Take a group of "gifted" middle schoolers fueled by hormones and insecurities and pair them with a first-year teacher. Most would expect pandemonium or disorganization, at best. However, Ms. Gibson recognized gifts in each of us that were more than test scores. She also taught us to recognize the qualities in others and to appreciate our differences. It takes a special individual to teach an insecure, awkward 8th grader to laugh at herself, laugh with others, and have fun in the moment. Ms. Gibson brought out those qualities in my classmates and myself. I don't remember much about test scores that year. I'm sure they were well above average, but I clearly recall the laughter made, the friendships fostered, and the confidence gained.

Mary Ann Gibson—words can't explain the love I have for you, you taught me so many things and was there for me in so many ways!!! Every time I hear you speak my heart [gets] filled with so much joy because I know some of your story and I am truly glad to see your GLORY!!! You are so deserving of whatever GOD [has] for you, Dr. Mary Ann Gibson!!!

Today is your last day as a Houston County Educator. You are finally retiring this year. Yay! I can't thank God enough for placing such an amazing woman in my life, and I'm sure there are others who can say the same. I've never met someone so caring and so passionate about helping others. I've seen you touch many lives within Crawford County, and everyone values the love you showed because they know that it's real. Grandma, I am so proud of you. From a custodian to Dr. Gibson! You're truly an inspiration. Now, let's celebrate!

I am so proud to call you my favorite teacher. I fell in love with math in elementary school because of you. The compassion you showed toward your students and your work were very inspiring. Your caring and loving personality allowed you to treat each student as your own child. I want to give you your flowers today and say, "Thank you," and "I love you."

Dr. Gibson was a role model to her students and a trusted confidant to her colleagues. She played such a crucial role in shaping the lives of her students because she wasn't just interested in them while they were in her classroom, she kept in touch with her students and their parents long after they exited her class. Through her knowledge, patience, and love, Dr. Gibson gave a strong shape to her students' whole lives. Dr. Gibson shared her academic knowledge, ethical values, and assimilated moral values into her classroom which helped shape her student's personalities and made them better human beings!

Ms. Gibson: a true lover of education. You always taught me about life! I loved having the mock trials in the classroom. It gave everyone a chance to resolve their differences, no matter what race. You were not only my teacher, but a big mother figure in my life. I am truly blessed to know and to love you. Thank you for everything!

As a current educator myself, I know how important it is to establish positive relationships with all stakeholders, especially students and their families. That's what we received upon arrival in Ms. Gibson's class in eighth grade! It was an instant feeling of belonging! From every lesson, high-five, and even hug, Ms. Gibson made every child feel welcome. Although she was small in stature, she spoke boldly, commanding the attention of anyone when needed. Her encouragement and unmatched love were quite large for each student and was on display every day. There are too many memories to share, but one of my fondest memories of Ms. Gibson's classroom was her allowing us to work collaboratively with each other because she knew that [we] were a group of students who had and would always continue to push each other to greatness. In other words, she allowed us to be instrumental in our own learning, thus creating a student-centered classroom. She will never know how much she meant to many students. I love Ms. Mary Ann Gibson, a true gem to have ever [graced the halls] of Crawford County Schools.

My life's journey has been an extraordinary odyssey, beginning with the scorching and relentless Georgia sun beating down on me as I toiled in the fields as a sharecropper. Alongside my hardworking parents, I spent long, hard days picking cotton and peaches, with the sweat on our brows matching the rhythm of our labor. If you've been there, then you know what that's like.

As we worked in the fields, unbeknownst to us, the planes would appear out of nowhere, flying low and overhead to irrigate the crops. In their wake, we would find ourselves unexpectedly drenched as well. We received no warning that the planes were coming. Little did I know that this humble beginning would set the stage for a remarkable transformation.

Through determination and an unrelenting spirit, I chose the path toward education and personal growth that would eventually lead me to stand tall and proud to receive my hard-earned doctorate degree. With each step I took toward my goals, the weight of the past fueled my determination. And so, on that momentous day as I walked across that hallowed stage, a sense of accomplishment washed over me, leaving me emotional, humbled, and grateful for the opportunities that life had presented.

Yet the road that led me there was far from smooth. It was marked by many unexpected twists and turns, both exhilarating and challenging. At times, it seemed as if disappointment lurked around every corner and threatened to extinguish the flame of hope that was within me. There were many times when I wanted to quit, to let the forces against me win.

It was during those moments of despair that from out of nowhere came resilience I didn't know I had. My faith in God pushed me forward when everything seemed insurmountable. Among the disappointments, there were also moments of unbridled joy that fueled my spirit and helped guide me toward my purpose. Each accomplishment, no matter how big or small, became a cause for celebration, reminding me that continued determination could really transform dreams into reality if I could just keep going.

I did my job and I know that I did it very well. In the beginning, I promised myself that I wouldn't be a teacher and fail to touch the life of at least one student. I kept my promise. And now, as I reflect on the profound journey that brought me to this very moment, I find myself embracing a new chapter—one where the power of my experiences and the lessons I learned along the way have inspired me to take pen to paper to compose my journey and my family story into a compelling book.

With this book, I strive to inspire and uplift, to share the triumphs and tribulations that have shaped me into the person I am today. It is my hope that others, regardless of their circumstances, will find hope and humor within these pages and recognize that the human spirit can overcome any obstacle and soar to unimaginable heights.

As I look ahead to the next chapter of my life, I carry with me the lessons learned from my journey—a reminder that determination and faith in God can transform the ordinary into the extraordinary. Our past does not define us, but it can certainly propel us toward greatness. Take it from me, the lady who started off in the fields picking cotton and peaches who then eked out a minimal living as a maid and a janitor, and who eventually earned a doctorate degree, even if my professional colleagues did refuse to call me "Doctor."

I hope that I effectively conveyed a vital message that I believe is essential to share. Most readers of this book likely have not had an easy start in life. Life's challenges often begin from the moment we arrive on this planet. The teacher that is within me would like to encourage you. My hope is to uplift you and to reassure you that you are already equipped to reach remarkable heights.

The highly distinguished Harvard- and Duke-University-educated psychologist, *New York Times* Bestselling Author, professor at Pepperdine University, and first African American President of the American Psychological Association, Dr. Thema Bryant, in her book, *Homecoming: Overcome Fear and Trauma to Reclaim Your Whole, Authentic Self,* tells a wonderful Liberian fable about an eagle.

This eagle was raised on a farm with chickens, and having been so reared, it had no notion of its great majesty. Having been told many times by an expert of its mighty power to soar high in the open skies, the eagle still could not comprehend itself as anything other than a barnyard bird like the other chickens on the farm. Exasperated that the eagle could not be convinced by mere words, the expert finally took matters into his own hands. He gathered the eagle and climbed to the roof of the barn. There, he told the eagle that he understood how all its life it had been told it was a chicken, and that it should just behave like all other chickens. The eagle, tired of the expert's assertions about its prowess, spread its wings and soared. The eagle found its authentic self and was never again found among the chickens.

Like the eagle, I hope that everyone reading this book will also find their true selves, regardless of past influences or challenging circumstances that might have somehow dimmed their brilliance.

Andrew and two of his sons

*Andrew, my son. The wind beneath my wings.
(Retired jersey; football, baseball, and basketball star)*

*Solomon, my riding partner; went
to college before he went to school.*

Andrew's daughter babysitting his twin grandsons

Andrew's son and daughter

Author at her Retirement Ceremony

Author wearing Lola's Sweater

Author, in graduation regalia

Author's brothers_from left_Jimmy, Johnny, Chuck

Author's Father

Catherine at school event in poodle skirt

Chair students gave author for Mother's Day one year

Family Photo

My beautiful mother 1934-2023

*My brother Chuck, who now has three daughters,
five grandchildren, and a lovely wife.*

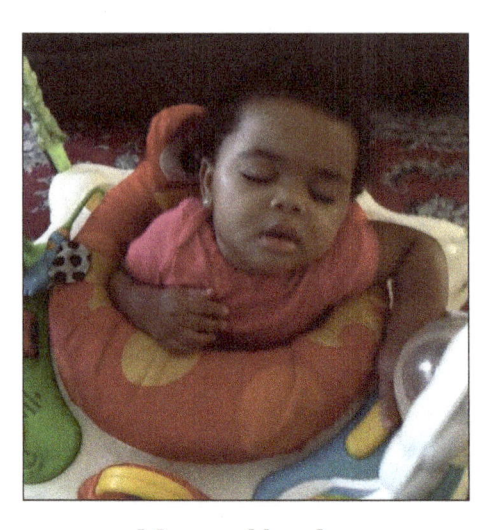

My granddaughter

My granddaughter wearing her tiara

My grandson at his graduation

My grandson, one of Andrew's son

My lovely Grandmother Gertrude

My lovely mother at her birthday celebration

My lovely sister Minnie

My mother and my children at a family gathering

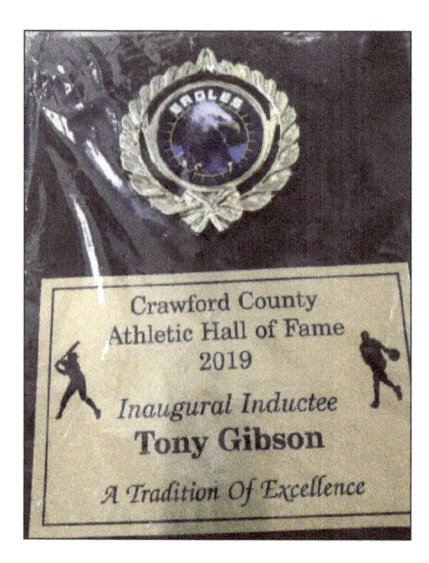

My son's Baseball Hall of Fame plaque

My son's retired baseball jacket sleeve

*Right to left Chuck, Larry, and Jason.
(Jason's wife is my wonderful sister-in-law whom
I love dearly, along with my nieces and nephews)*

Donnie (That ball is still in the air today!)

Right to Left, Murphy and Larry

Rita, my daughter

Jimmy's wife (my sister-in-law. Mother of three sons, one deceased) and my daughter, Rita

If by any chance I fall, I've been there already!
- Dr. Mary Ann Gibson, Ed.D. (2023)

Milton Keynes UK
Ingram Content Group UK Ltd.
UKHW052004041223
433768UK00001B/19

9 798822 927414